MW01298134

"With elegant simplicity, Kathryn Ford reveals that there is an in
separable bond between mind, body and spirit that directly affects our
health and well-being. The prescription she has written for all of us is that
the secrets to achieving radical healing are contained within her 7-step
system. I highly recommend this book to anyone who wants to make the
rest of their life the best of their life."

– Mary Morrissey

"Find a person who is getting the results you want, ask for their advice
and then do exactly what they tell you to do. That has worked wonders for
me for many years. Kathryn Ford is happy, healthy and wealthy. She be-
lieves self-care is the new healthcare and the largest component of self-care
is self-love. This book is a must-read for anyone wanting to live a life of
full-spectrum wealth."

– Bob Proctor

"Kathryn Ford's Be Well! offers tender healing for any sense of un-
worthiness or lack of self-love, and invites us into a revolution in consciousness through the acceptance of our hearts' inherent knowing that
each of us is, in essence, wholeness itself."

– Michael Bernard Beckwith

"Kathryn Ford is a joyous and radiant woman. Her energy is contagious, and her teachings profound. In her brilliant and inspiring book she
teaches how the body's own pharmacy will release naturally healing and
healthful chemicals to support our vitality and well-being. She shares key
concepts to revitalize every cell."

-Diana von Welanetz Wentworth

i

BE WELL!

A 7-Step System
for Radical
Healing

Kathryn Ford

A FREE Gift for You!

5 Keys to Discovering Your Personal Expression of Self Love

Simply visit http://www.freewellnessgift.com

Dedication

Each of these pages has been written for you and for all those who have touched your heart, and you theirs. We all have an unlimited ocean of love within us that runs as deep as our hearts will allow.

Table of Contents

Foreword by
Bernie Siegel, MD

My first thought, as I write this foreword, is that in Kathryn Ford's book, the term "radical healing" should be interpreted as profound healing. The wisdom Kathryn shares with us through her book's wisdom is profound and about the potential which exists in each of us and should be seen as a form of natural healing we are all capable of; though, because of our past and the messages many of us were exposed to as we grew up, it may seem radical because it is very profound and not the experience we are taught to expect. I have learned that what occurs when people recover from an illness is not really spontaneous. It happens when people make changes in their lives and find self-love and harmony. The healing occurs because our emotions affect our internal chemistry and the body responds to the message of the will to live and a new life. I call it self-induced healing. It comes when we bring love into our lives through self-transformation and experience love for our bodies and our new life.

It is an age-old message and filled with lessons to be learned, but it is far better to learn them from the wisdom and experience of Kathryn and the wisdom of the great teachers than it is to be learned from a personal disaster. You will find the greatest life coaches all share similar themes because they have all seen them work and lead to healing. The problem is that you have to show up for practice and not fear failure and, therefore, not even attempt to heal. I know the truth from my experience as a doctor, and I do not allow the negative beliefs or fears of others stop me from participating in my life and attempt to heal and be well. Everyone who heals in a so-called "radical way" has a story to tell about why it happened and we can all learn from their stories.

It is interesting to me that Kathryn created a seven-step system because seven is a very symbolic number. Every religion has seven days in its week while varying numbers of days in its monthly calendar. And remember how many days it took God to create our world. Seven speaks about a cycle, and when we complete that cycle in a healthy way, it leads us into a new life of self-creation and our authentic life truly begins as we are born again. The eighth day then becomes our new beginning and new life.

While I am writing this what came into my head, as we try to help you, is the fact that life is beyond understanding. Creation is not something anyone can explain. We are all here getting an education, just as we did when we went to school. The problem is that we will all be tested along the way and that is when things can become difficult. Reading about the experiences of those who are now post-graduate students of life, by passing all the tests they encountered, can enlighten all of us and reveal what radical healing can offer. I repeat that we all have the potential, when we abandon the wounds of our past and the negative hypnotic messages and effects of the authority figures in our lives, to move on.

We need to accept our self-worth and that we are all God's children. Create shrines around your home containing pictures of yourself as a child and love that kid. You can reparent yourself and be grateful for the opportunity life presents you with. A childhood filled with indifference, rejection, and abuse, the opposites of love, can make it difficult, but you can change. When you bring gratitude, love, humor, and relationships into your life, you change your internal chemistry and ability to heal. Grace, faith, and accepting God's love is a different kind of medicine which changes our internal chemistry. Joy is a choice. You are in control of one thing: your thoughts. You can change your attitude or your life and reap the benefits of the change.

Kathryn writes about oceans of wellness, while I talk to people about the still pond. I know from my medical experience what the quiet mind, free of fears and negativity, can do. In various myths, the still pond reflects the truth and is where the ugly duckling sees he is a swan, and a tiger raised by goats sees—for the first time—he is really a tiger. The duckling doesn't resent his mother and the tiger doesn't grieve his mother's death; they live in the moment. So quiet your mind and see the truth about yourself and your life. Turbulent minds and water reveal nothing which is helpful to us. When the internal anger and turbulence persist, we attack ourselves as auto-immune diseases demonstrate to us.

Think about attending *Excellence Institute*, another of Kathryn's concepts and fearing, as most people do, that you will fail because you do not meet your definition of being excellent. What is excellence and who is? We all have the potential to be excellent, and we need to define it in a healthy way and stop fearing the opportunity by seeking help and coaching and accepting it so you can improve and do an excellent job with the life you have been given. Kathryn doesn't speak about something that I and other health care professionals know exists. Immune-competent personalities are people who have the personality which helps them to stay healthy, heal, and survive. They are not submissive sufferers, but responsible participants in their own lives, expressing their needs and desires while living authentically, and not the life imposed upon them by the authority figures in their life.

As Helen Keller said, "Vibrant health isn't about your body but about your life and attitude." Kathryn talks about disruptions in our lives. I find this theme over and over again when people talk about the interruptions in their work and lives. They all find enlightenment when they realize the disruptions and interruptions are what our lives are truly about. They are the teachers in our school of life. Coaches confront our performance in order to improve it. They do not belittle, demean, and make negative statements about us. They instruct and improve us. So read on and learn from Kathryn, and let her enlighten you. Just as hunger leads you to nourishment, and charcoal under pressure becomes a diamond, your curse can become your teacher and blessing.

When you love yourself, your life, and your body, you stop being a submissive sufferer and people pleaser and feel free to display appropriate anger when you are not treated with respect. You understand that it makes no sense to wait until you are close to death to choose life and give birth to a new life and self due to your life's labor pains. You will find that when you feel you are worth giving birth to, that the labor pains don't hurt as much. How do you decide what is right for you? You let your heart make up your mind. Pay attention to your feelings and you will find the right path to follow. When you choose life, wonderful things happen and they are not coincidences. You made it occur by your choices. We prepare our futures unconsciously. Seeking coaches to direct you makes a difference too.

When you are sailing on the ocean of wellness, take notice of the rhythm and unity of the waves. They make beautiful sounds when they strike the shore, just as streams do running over stones. They don't complain about what has been placed in their way. They make use of and accept all that lies before them. Yes, they can become tsunamis too, but we have the choice as to what form and use our water takes. Our healthy desires, intentions and relationships will guide us to self-induced healing.

The medical profession needs to learn from success and realize good results are not spontaneous, but are accomplished through the work of the individual. We need to not treat the result but also the cause. Centenarians share four common traits: relationships with a group, healthy diet, physical activity, and purpose. You can accomplish this by listening to yourself and your body and not just living with a diagnosis, but living an experience and healing any negative components in your life which are a part of your experience.

Keep a journal of your feelings and meditate so you are aware of what is experienced and stored within you. Choose life, and self-healing will occur along with the wonderful coincidences I mentioned. Emotional hunger and surrender can become your teachers. Stop fighting a war against your enemies and seek to heal your life and create peace. Waging battles and wars empowers your enemy and wastes your energy. Seeking peace, love, and healing has the opposite effect.

Do not judge yourself harshly as you undertake the change. You are a work in progress and, as a portrait painter, I like to think of myself as a blank canvas upon which a work of art is being created. I also realize if I do not like the look of the painting, I can correct it when it doesn't reveal the truth as the still pond does. I truly learned a lot from my self-portrait—all covered up in a surgical cap, mask, and gown—and what I needed to uncover in my life. Remember there is always more color on the palette and what we control are our thoughts. So create a mantra you repeat throughout the day by combining a group of sayings, which can reprogram your thoughts and empower you at all times and in any circumstances.

Kathryn pointed out the importance of the number three to her. I think it represents the trinity and is significant. I think it is no coincidence our TV set uses the number three to make all channels available to us. Numbers have meaning, and we use them as symbols to store memories also. When people do drawings and a number appears, and you ask them if that number means anything to them, their answers are always about meaningful and usually painful events in their lives. It just proves how we store our life within our bodies. Even organ transplants verify this fact. Memories go with the transplanted organ into the donor recipient's memory.

Remember that happiness is a choice and that a perfect world would be meaningless and not creation. We are here to live and learn. Think of yourself as having two role models I prefer to use, water and animals. The water is capable of change and can present itself as a solid, liquid, or vapor. We are capable of change too, but we are not complete as animals are as we are still learning. So find your role models and rehearse and practice until you become the person you want to be through your radical self-induced healing.

My last test for you is to ask you how you will introduce yourself to God when you get to Heaven? If you don't want to be told to come back when you know who you are, the correct answer is for you to realize that you are not separated from the divine, and say "I am your child" or "It is You." Never forget your self-worth. You are more significant than to identify yourself by a role like mother, wage earner, or doctor. You decide your true identity and not others. My parable is that you are a satellite dish, remote control, and TV screen. Many channels are available to you, so use your mind to select the proper one, like a remote control, and your body to demonstrate it and display it just as a TV screen reveals the content of the performance for all to see. Just be sure you tune into the channel which helps you to choose life and find your authentic life and self which you can have faith in and benefits all of creation.

Introduction

Each and every one of us has some sort of dis-ease in our life. Whether it is a physical illness, challenges with relationships and love, financial stress, or something that simply takes away some of the "ease" in life. One thing I know for sure is that we are complex spiritual beings having a human experience and everything going on in our life affects our health, well-being and our ability to maintain youthfulness. But, no matter what your challenge is, I have found the answers to living a life of excellence. The good news is, despite the onslaught of challenges that may come our way, we can shine in the midst of them and transform our life! Your best life, one that is filled with health and well-being, doesn't have to be a dream any longer. Through the following pages, I have the privilege of sharing my own dis-eases and experiences with you. My aim is to shed light on some proven ways that we can overcome our challenges and embark on the most incredible journey possible.

Over the years, I have come to understand that my true purpose in life is to inspire and empower others. As someone who has lived with serious health challenges for over half my life, I want nothing more than to help those who may also be facing health challenges of their own. A life full of love and joy is not only possible, but is something that you deserve.

For nearly three decades, I have lived with neuromyelitis optica (NMO), which is similar to multiple sclerosis, but considered to be far more serious. But what I can tell you now, and what will be apparent throughout the rest of this book, is that my own dis-ease has helped me discover how incredible and fulfilling life can be. My path has led me to overcome many challenges in order to not only be well, but to *thrive*. Instead of simply coping with their symptoms, it is one of my greatest desires in life to help others make the rest of their life the best of their life.

By having this book in your hands, you are sending an important message out into the world—I am ready for my life to change for the better. Well, I am here to tell you, excitement and peace are around the corner.

My main purpose with these pages is to pass along all that I have learned so that you can accelerate your own road towards wellness. From my difficulties, successes, and the trials and errors I have pushed through, an understanding of how to succeed in the face of dis-ease has been pushed to the forefront. So take my hand, and let's make your life everything you could have ever dreamed it to be!

Who Is Kathryn Ford?

Let me take just a moment to introduce myself and share a little bit about my work in the world. I am an award-winning master life coach and consultant, international speaker, and author. I am the founder and president of *Excellence Institute,* the premier training center for living a life of excellence. I have had the pleasure of receiving continuing education from the *Coaching in Leadership and Healthcare* conference sponsored by Harvard Medical School, and I am a member of their *Institute of Coaching Professional Association.*

In my practice, I specialize in achieving health and well-being and maintaining youthfulness. Through my coaching programs, I teach the essential tools and methods for living a life of full-spectrum wealth. This means living life with an abundance of health and well-being, and maintaining youthfulness, rich relationships, and time and money freedom—truly a life of excellence!

While reading this book, I hope that you can approach it in the same way that I approach my daily life—with an attitude that is ready to have fun! Your spirit loves fun, so for the sake of your health and well-being, I am going to prescribe you a full dose of daily fun! By infusing your life with laughter, joy, and smiles, you are telling your health that it is a priority to you.

This was not always the case for me. My own health was compromised after receiving the diagnosis of a severe autoimmune dis-ease. Looking back, I can see that much of the development of this dis-

8

ease was inspired by my physical and mental environments. But, despite some difficulties along the way, I am thrilled to say that I have moved through the diagnosis and have created an extraordinary lifestyle in the process. My hope is that my words and my experiences can help you move through your own challenges with grace.

Even though there was a time in my life where I wasn't sure that things would ever get better, it feels amazing to be sharing the secrets I have uncovered, and to tell you that your life can be amazing. Together, we are going to go on a journey that will teach us to have the courage to allow our inner lights to shine bright.

I can say this without a shadow of doubt—the work I am doing now is my true purpose in life. The clouds of uncertainty have passed, and the world is full of possibility. As the well-known words say, "The sun is always shining, we need only remove the clouds."

The work I do and the words I share are meant for everyone. Whether you are struggling with a scary diagnosis or wanting to make your health and well-being a priority, this book is for you. My clients come from many different backgrounds, and they have applied the secrets I am sharing with you now to every area of their lives. Whether you are facing a serious health challenge or craving a life of excellence, I am so glad to meet you!

You Deserve to Feel Healthy

You may be thinking that you can't do this whole "self-care" thing because you have been "this or that" for so long and it is all you know. Or, maybe, you have lived with your dis-ease for so long that you feel stuck. For many people, they feel like they don't deserve love and happiness. Well, if you feel that any of those conditions apply to you, you are not alone. Many people who first come to my practice have had these thoughts at one time or another. I even had them myself. With that being said, I am here to tell you that these thoughts and feelings can be overcome!

Through patience and practice, I have found that it all comes down to the area between our ears—our mindsets and the thoughts we allow to take up residence. Our thoughts have power, so we will take a deep dive into ways that we can shape them to benefit us and create the kind of lifestyle we have dreamt of.

Disruption Was the Theme of My Life

I have had a great deal of disruptions in my life. From health challenges to problems in my closest personal relationships, the way hasn't always been easy. As I look back, I can see that there was a theme of not respecting or loving myself. This was a pattern of mine, one that far too many people will be familiar with. My natural tendency as an emotionally sensitive person often made it so I was deeply hurt by criticism or mean-spirited remarks.

The criticism I received may not have impacted someone else in the same debilitating way it did for me. I would often hear, "You're just too sensitive." While this initially led me to feel bad about my sensitivity, it also gave rise to an opportunity to transform myself into the person I wanted to be. Not only did this enhance my relationships, but it also made me a stronger and more resilient person than I had ever been before.

In fact, I can now see that my sensitive nature is one of my greatest gifts, and I hold onto it dearly. It allows me to be loving, compassionate, and sensitive towards others.

However, before I understood the gifts my sensitivity held, it was difficult to see it in a positive light. In hindsight, I can see these negative thought patterns were so ingrained in me that I allowed myself to believe the criticism was true. As a result, I began attacking myself with self-criticisms.

My body responded in turn. It was only a matter of time before I experienced the first symptoms of physical illness in 1989. I am now able to take full responsibility for allowing myself to harbor and internalize the criticism I heard. By believing that I was not deserving, those beliefs spiraled out of control and contributed to my physical illness. Belief and outcome are intricately intertwined.

Love Brings Power

I now know that the most important person to love Kathryn Ford with unconditional, undying love is Kathryn Ford. Realizing your own importance and putting yourself first leads to a place of peace and unbounded love—both for you and rippling from you!

We each have a mind, a physical self, and a spiritual self. By honoring each part of ourselves, we can find total well-being. I am continuously asking for Divine help in realizing my own strength and ability to decide what kind of life I want to be living. We can learn to empower ourselves by listening to the sweet, small voice that all of us hold within ourselves. By listening, taking action, and boldly stepping into the realm of infinite possibility, we honor our own potential and ability to change the world.

Your Journey is Underway

I could share all of my own experiences and hope that they shed some light on your personal challenges, but that isn't enough. I want to equip you with tools and strategies that will lead you to a healthier and more magnificent you. No matter the challenges you are facing or are going to face, I want to walk side-by-side with you on a journey that will ultimately allow you to find happiness. Every life has potential to be vibrant, and we have so much opportunity to thrive through our struggles and successes.

I strive to focus on expecting the best while having confidence in my ability to navigate through any challenges that might crop up. One key I have found very helpful to my own vibrant health is my belief that I am called to share what I have learned. I want my own understanding to help others facing similar challenges to the ones I worked through. All of the tools provided will lay a foundation for you to build on. Your journey is going to be reflective of your experiences and your unique personality. By utilizing the provided tools, you can tailor your life in a way that is nothing short of brilliant!

The Key to Thriving (According to Kathryn Ford)

In order to maintain your health and well-being as a priority, you have to be number one. Caring for yourself and understanding your importance and value fills you to the brim with love and capability. Designing a routine of drawing love and joy inward makes sharing those same virtues all the much more powerful. You don't have to settle for a life of surviving; you can choose to *thrive*. You are worth it, and the quality of your life matters.

If you want your body to function at its highest capacity, these pages are for you. Small changes can often lead to big results! From taking some time each day to be pampered, to surrounding yourself with the right people, your energy quotient and the quality of your life can increase by leaps and bounds.

We are going to look at the keys to a life of full-spectrum wealth. Not only are we going to discuss the tools you should be using, but we will also go into depth on the importance of removing negative energy from your life. I can't wait to share this journey with you. So, let's get started!

WAVE ONE
SELF-CARE

I believe that self-care is the new healthcare. As my own success stories prove, learning to practice self-care on a routine basis can help you achieve the most incredible health and well-being that you can imagine. The pleasure of following through and feeling better than ever—both physically and emotionally—is very much worth it. So just do it! You are worth the investment in yourself.

By practicing the art and science of self-care, you will bathe every cell in your body in the beautiful chemicals released by your own inner pharmacy. Just imagine now what that renewing feels like. And, since our minds and bodies are connected in such an intimate way, simply by thinking about the potential of increased self-care, you are already jumping into my program, OCEANS OF WELLNESS˚ - A Fountain of Youth. Go ahead! Try thinking of drifting into something like a long, relaxing massage as one of your own self-care practices. Can you experience how soothing that feels to your muscles? It is a wonderful way to take your life back!

A New Healthcare

In This Chapter

* Finding our true nature and pouring love into ourselves
* Listening to our body and recognizing its gentle nudgings

> 66 *We must first learn to fall so deeply in love with ourselves that our very nature is to take care of our physical, emotional, and spiritual needs.* 99
>
> – Kathryn Ford

When I first started writing this book, I heavily considered the following title: *Saving My Body, Finding Myself.* Underneath everything I was learning, and all of the steps that I was taking to maximize the quality of my life, I realized that the ultimate purpose for my journey was to find myself. And yet, after all the trials and difficulties along the way, this grand adventure has proven itself to have a purpose far more expansive and incredible than I could have ever imagined. Not only was I able to find myself, but I also learned how to *intimately know and live true to myself* in everything I did.

Coming to terms with these truths would have been an incredible adventure with nothing else added, but there was an additional step to my journey. While searching for remedies to help my ailing body, I was finding answers that were revealing my true self; even though I may not have always been aware of it, I was searching for my true well-being every step of the way. With great excitement, I can share some good news—I found it! And that makes the purpose of this book, my intent with each and every word, to help you find your own wellness, your own true well-being.

Merriam Webster's definition of well-being is as follows: "*The state of being well, happy, or prosperous.*" While that definition creates a vague outline, I don't think it describes wellness in its truest state. For me, the state of being well relates to our entire being. In my own quest, I find myself coming back to my personal definition of well-being: *Developing an emotional state of happiness that creates an emotional state of well-being, which in turn will bring about a physical state of increased well-being. In turn, this creates a trinity of power to generate a full-spectrum life.* As each of these qualities swell in our lives, the next begins to grow in size, leading to a cycle that causes our happiness and well-being to blossom each and every day.

This book is filled with many personal discoveries. These discoveries have uncovered many useful tools for you to apply to different areas of your life. I suggest you try the ones that speak to you and evaluate their effectiveness in your own life. Maintain those that are working for you, and let go of those that are not in order to make room for the next practice that intrigues and inspires you.

By continuously evaluating and re-evaluating the practices promoting your own personal well-being, it is safe to say that you are allowing yourself to connect with the ones best suited for specific times in your life. At any given moment, we are all at different places on our journeys. I have found with my clients; an individualized approach has the greatest impact. I encourage you to take the information provided in this book and customize it to your own path. It is my wish to champion you as you embark on the journey of a lifetime, becoming the best version of yourself through a careful application of the practices we explore.

I want to make a special note that everything we discuss is about the science of *being* well. After all I have been through, living my best life has come down to unconditionally loving myself and living fearlessly! This way of living promotes the optimal health and well-being I want for each and every one of us. In order to put this well-being into practice, we will need the necessary tools and support to adopt a lifestyle where we can discover the oceans of possibility within ourselves!

The Powerful Role of Self-Care

Self-care is the new healthcare. I think that everyone would agree that taking care of our bodies is incredibly important, and looking after our mental well-being takes care of the physical in turn. I feel that self-care needs to be an overarching priority and focus for every one of us. In fact, it is the foundation of my entire practice at *Excellence Institute,* and is the representation of a journey into healing your body through self-care and self-love.

Each of the subsequent portions of this book supports the overarching section on self-care we are about to dive into. If you look at gratitude, peace, self-worth, grace, and joy, they are all covered under the encompassing umbrella of self-care. The waves we cover within this book—each one providing tools for different areas of our lives— are a subset of self-care, with the largest component of self-care being self-love.

In order to allow self-care a place in your daily life, it is necessary to understand that taking special care of yourself and determining what nourishes you physically, mentally, emotionally, and spiritually is *not selfish*. In fact, it is a mandatory requirement if we are to thrive and live a life of excellence. I have a calendar in my office that the great author and publisher, Louise Hay, puts out each year. Every page contains an inspiration for its corresponding day of the year, ensuring 365 days of affirmation. One of my favorites reads, "I listen to my body and lovingly respond to its needs - giving it just the right amount of food, rest, and exercise." This is a perfect reminder to inspire us each and every day of our lives!

Experiencing The True Me

A Healthy Dose of Daily Love

66 *There is only one thing that heals every problem and that is to love yourself.* 99

–Louise Hay

Now, before we jump into the art and science of self-care any further, I would like you to answer the following question by writing it out in a journal: "I am so happy and grateful now that ..." and then finish it by detailing the best possible life and all of the desires you can imagine.

As you write, make sure to focus on feelings of gratitude; from personal experience, I can assure you that these feelings can be incredibly powerful. For example, let me begin by saying, "I am so happy and grateful that we are focused on my favorite topic, which just so happens to be health and the art and science of self-care."

It was George Washington Carver that said, "If you fall in love with something deeply, it will reveal its secrets to you." So I did just that. I fell in love with health and well-being, as well as the art and science of self-care.

Stemming from the truth of George Washington Carver's words, it was then that those secrets were revealed to me and why I know that the largest component of self-care is undoubtedly self-love. I firmly believe the ability to extend unconditional love to ourselves is paramount to living a life of excellence.

It is my personal belief that our health and well-being depends on self-love. A physician once said, "The best medicine for humans is love." Someone asked, "What if it doesn't work?" He smiled and said, "Increase the dose." Now that is a prescription I can certainly embrace!

Now, one of the ways that I personally relate to the word love, is through this acronym:

L. Life Giving

O. OCEANS OF WELLNESS˙

V. Vibrant Health

E. Excellence in Living

Life Giving – OCEANS OF WELLNESS˙ – for – Vibrant Health – and – Excellence in Living

I am a firm believer that extending a deep, pure love to ourselves precipitates happiness. And happy means healthy! For example, scores of studies link happiness to a wide range of tangible benefits, such as a lessened likelihood of stroke, better resistance to colds and an increased immune function, greater resilience to adversity, less physical pain, lower cortisol levels, and less overall stress and inflammation.

These last points are extremely significant to not only our health, but also our well-being. With regards to happiness, research shows about 40-percent of our level of happiness is actually within our own control. Now isn't that encouraging? Think about it, have you ever experienced so much joy and happiness that you felt it in every cell of your body? I am certain we have all felt that at one time or another.

In fact, happiness goes even deeper than that, reaching all the way to your genes. Barbara Fredrickson, Ph.D. and lead author of an important study relating to love, found that not all things that feel good offer the same benefits on a cellular level.

I had the pleasure and opportunity to be a student of Dr. Fredrickson while attending a Harvard Medical School conference. While there, I learned that the research work she and others have been doing along the lines of love, especially as it relates to our health, is overwhelmingly supportive when looking at the power of love in our lives.

In Dr. Fredrickson's recent findings, she reveals that different types of happiness affect human genomes in dramatically different ways, potentially having significant implications on our physical health and well-being.

She states that there are two major types of happiness: one is "being in the moment" (taking in a gorgeous sunset or eating a mouth-watering piece of chocolate), and the other is similar to the buzz we get from "having a higher purpose" (being of service to others and experiencing a connection with those around us).

While both of these types of happiness reinforce each other, studies have shown that we certainly don't want to be without the latter. I am a firm believer that a connection to a higher purpose *must be a priority* if we want to truly be well and live a life of excellence!

Connected to Something Larger than Ourselves

One of my favorite "to do's" I prescribe my clients is to actively ride the wave of helping or supporting someone else. I find the benefits of this prescription are magnified when we, ourselves, may be in the midst of a challenge of our own. It is particularly important for living a life of excellence that we make regular use of this practice as a complement to following our individual purpose in life.

Even though it can be difficult to remember, this is especially important when times are most challenging. Remembering our higher purpose and *actively* helping others allows us to connect, or dial in, to the feeling that we are a part of something larger than ourselves. Believe me when I say that the calmness and security that comes as a result can be truly life changing and health enhancing.

What speaks to me about this practice is the constant reminder that wherever we go, there we are. This not only causes us to make ourselves a priority within our respective lives, but requires that we embrace the role of being our own best friend. We can then bathe in the kind of friendship that is unwavering and everlasting, reveling as it pours the power of love completely over our mind, body, and spirit. Not only does this refresh our beings, but it grants us a new kind of power. Among so many gifts we have the ability to give, this is perhaps the greatest one that we can extend to ourselves.

The divine nature of love is what allows us to feel safe, nurtured, and supported. There is nothing in the world quite like it. Love will do more for your health and well-being than anything else you can imagine. John Clarke said, "True love is the joy of life."

The necessity of love is visible in all aspects of our lives. For the sake of our health, we must love ourselves unconditionally. To excel at our work, we must love what we do. And, if you don't, change it and do something else. With respect to our relationships, we must love the people that share the human experience with us.

Finally, if we find that we are experiencing toxic behaviors from someone else, it is important to create distance and/or move on and focus on healthy relationships.

The Physical Impact of Relationships

I know this is sometimes easier said than done, but who we associate with is critical to our health. Relationships cellularize in our bodies and have a direct impact on our health and well-being. But the first and most important relationship starts with loving ourselves. We must learn to fall so deeply in love with ourselves that our very nature is to take care of our physical, emotional, and spiritual needs.

For example, if releasing body weight is something we want to do—it being an expression of loving our physical and emotional bodies—the way we look at the process makes all the difference. Instead of saying, "I can't have that piece of pizza because I am on a diet," a healthy, loving way of approaching it would be, "I choose to make a healthier choice because I deserve the best for my life and healthy choices are a way of extending love to myself." Notice how the initial statement carries an energy that screams deprivation while the healthy approach focuses on accepting your own love?

In my case, it is loving my body that causes me to make a nutritious, low-calorie, low-carbohydrate, gluten-free choice. In addition, the evidence that gluten is not healthy for those of us with an autoimmune diagnosis helps me extend love to my body by not filling it with something that would cause it harm.

Bathing Our Cells in the Energy of Love

When we make a small shift in our mindset for how we approach healthy choices—whether it's about food, exercise, or any number of things—we can improve our health. If we simply change the way we look at it and shift the words we use, we completely transform the vibration surrounding the decision. Now, we bathe our cells in love, which feels infinitely better than deprivation. Love is a phenomenal emotion!

Make it a practice to be a vibrational match for self-love. This involves getting into the energy current of LOVE. Do whatever it takes to live your life and operate from a place that keeps you rooted in giving and receiving your own love. No longer will you need to push against the things you don't want, don't like, or don't agree with, since this only causes us to fall out of alignment with the things we really care about, including vibrant health and well-being.

When we push up against something, we press ourselves out of alignment with the very things that we are seeking. I remember a time when Mother Theresa was asked to participate in a demonstration against war. She declined, stating that they should contact her when they planned a march for peace. This beautifully illustrates the difference between pushing against something versus getting into alignment with the things that you truly want in your life. The trick is to match the energy and vibration of the reality you desire.

Every day, I practice this truth on my own health and well-being. As you know, part of my health history includes being diagnosed with a serious autoimmune dis-ease. Years later, I would uncover that it had been misdiagnosed and was actually a much more serious condition called Neuromyelitis Optica (or NMO). It became readily apparent that the need to get into alignment was necessary for the sake of my health.

The Opportunities and the Gifts

For every 100 people with multiple sclerosis (MS), only one person is diagnosed with NMO. I have always practiced integrative medicine and have adopted many holistic and alternative practices that support my journey in health. However, after learning of this new diagnosis, I made a critical decision. It was an opportunity and a gift to dive even deeper still and discover the well of power I have within me and one that we *all* have within us.

One of my practices during meditation is that of seeing, feeling, and believing myself to be in *perfect* health. It is a meditation that I believe every cell in my body loves to experience. I know in my heart, and my Higher Self has confirmed it, that LOVE is once again the answer. Since the beginning, I have always held the belief that just because I have a diagnosis, it does not have me! And just because I have been told that all these extremely frightening things *could* happen to me, does not mean they are going to or need to. Instead, I have the opportunity to place my focus on being healthy.

After receiving the news of my misdiagnosis, I went to Mayo Clinic in Rochester, Minnesota to see one of the world's leading experts on NMO. His first words to me were, "Are you Kathryn Ford? Wow, you don't even look like someone who has had MS for 22 years, let alone NMO. Please tell me, what else you are doing besides taking the medication that has been prescribed for your MS?"

His surprise was one of the biggest compliments I could receive! I shared with him all the integrative medicine tools and practices, including tapping into the power of my mind, that I had "prescribed" for myself. I also told him that my wellness prescriptions are ones that have only positive side effects and make me feel great. His response, "Don't stop any of that, because obviously it's working!" was music to my ears.

Checking my record and seeing that I had been taking every-other-day injections of a chemotherapy drug for MS, he asked when my next treatment would be. I told him I was giving it to myself that evening, to which he immediately said, "No, that medication is actually harmful to someone with NMO." After 16½ years of taking this drug, this was quite the blow.

I closed my eyes in shock; so many years of harmful "treatments" due to an incorrect diagnosis was a horrible thing to hear. But this wasn't the end to my story. I opened my eyes, looked right at him, and said, "I have a very powerful mind, and I believed those injections were helping me, so I know they did not hurt me." A huge sense of relief came over him and with a smile he said, "We are sticking with that! You really need to be sharing all this incredible information and the tools you have found through your 22 years of research with others!"

I would hear this same recommendation from two more doctors before I connected the dots which lead me to my true purpose in life. But for now, to make sure that my truth resonates loud and clear, know that I believe a healthy dose of love each day is the answer.

Regaining A Sense of Balance

“Be who you are and say what you feel, because those who mind don't matter and those who matter don't mind.”

– Dr. Seuss

Having looked at the importance of a daily dose of love, let's look at how to use your energy to improve your health. The secret here is to find *balance* in all areas of your life. Balance requires your own definition of what it means to you. Once you've come to your own understanding, you will notice when you are sliding into imbalance. This allows you the ability and momentum to gently redirect your present course towards one of true balance.

Learning to push your internal pause button to gently, and I emphasize the word gently, redirect your life towards balance is a form of art. Imbalance in life directly affects our health and well-being, period. One secret I have discovered to maintaining balance in my own life is to use what I call the "flight attendant analogy," one that we will look at in greater detail later. The core of the analogy is as follows:

Put your own mask on first and then assist those around you with theirs.

This is the perfect path to practicing the art and science of self-care, arrived at through a healthy dose of self-love.

As I look back on my life, many of the lessons I have learned revolve around balance in some way. For me, I must keep a constant watch over the amount of joy I allow into my life. I have struggled with depriving myself in the past and now keep a vigilant watch to ensure that never happens again.

Standing Outside of the Picture Frame

In recent years, it became readily apparent that I had struggled to recognize when I was allowing people, or situations, to rob me of my joy. Up until the misdiagnosis, I had a tendency to not look at my life from the "big picture" point of view.

But, what I have found is that it is far better to see individual situations from 10,000 feet up in order to grasp the overall effect people are having on my life. You may have heard how challenging it can be to see the picture when we are standing within the frame. Well, that is true!

When I do this, I am more readily able to evaluate two very important things. One, whether changes are needed in my life to restore balance, and two, how to avoid the pain that grows—or at least persists—when negative situations go unaddressed.

Much of life, both the good and the not-so-good, happens slowly over time. The challenge is to recognize when things are swaying too far in the wrong direction, so as not to adopt this as a new norm. Being able to take an honest look at your situation, and admitting when things are less than perfect, is the first step to moving forward in the healthiest manner possible.

A true awakening happened when I discovered even the most everyday parts of our lives needed to authentically reflect our nature and who we are. Carol Tuttle, an author of several well-known books and an acclaimed alternative psychotherapist, talks about the fact that energy is everywhere, and that even our wardrobe needs to be in balance with who we are.

She says, "Living contrary to your nature can make you sick. When we're true to our self, we sustain more life force energy." Included in Carol's focuses are, *Living Your Truth* and *Dressing Your Truth*. These are powerful ways to honor who we are, and to ultimately empower our desire to be true to ourselves.

Being true to myself and honoring myself have always been of significant importance to me. By including what I wear as part of the equation, I feel as though I am being true to my nature from the inside out!

Making Healthier Choices

With an illness or dis-ease (which is anything that causes us difficulty in our lives), it is imperative that you do all you can to function at your best with each individual system and segment of your life. And, even if you are absent of dis-ease in your body, it is necessary that you practice healthy choices to maintain true overall wellness moving forward.

When health conditions are present, we simply do not have the reserves available to rob another part of our body to make up for what we have lost. I often have clients with health challenges tell me that one of the real gifts of practicing true wellness has been that they are now healthier overall than ever before! A dis-ease is not who you are; even if it plays a part in your life, you can choose to overwhelm that segment with true wellness from every other angle.

The clients that have come to this realization watch their health more closely, make better and healthier decisions, and see their doctor for preventative practices. Simply put, they no longer take their health for granted. By choosing to live better and healthier than ever before, they are offering this precious gift for their complete and total well-being.

Managing Stress in Your Body

The most important factor in self-care is to learn how to effectively mitigate the kind of toxic stress that produces cortisol. It is impossible to avoid completely, but we do need to decrease the sources of stress in our lives, while at the same time adding richness in order to thrive and live a life of excellence.

Stress and anxiety can actually worsen the conditions we may already have, and in some instances exacerbate additional symptoms. Therefore, it is essential if we are already managing an existing health condition, that we do not accumulate additional challenges that may lead to decline or worsening as a result. There are several very effective tools available which, when practiced over time, make a significant impact on how we process stress. Again, it is impossible to avoid all stress in our lives. The way we perceive what is happening in our lives, and whether we develop positive habits or practices, can help us maintain inner peace regardless of what is happening in the outer world. The result of this thinking? A marked improvement on our overall physical health and well-being.

For instance, we can't just decide that the majority of our stress comes from relationships and then steer clear of them entirely. After all, life is all about relationships! But, some of them may require drastic measures to remove a person from our lives. That being said, with proper stress management practices in place and genuine attempts to work on the relationship, this does not always have to be the case.

Whatever the relationship, always remember that your health is at stake. And, if all other avenues are attempted and the stress level is still unacceptable, complete removal may be the only alternative.

Another important factor in the status of our health is what we put into our bodies. Unhealthy foods can put heavy wear on our systems and compound other stressors (such as the impact of the toxic relationships we just looked at). Even though my family always made healthy eating a priority, shortly after my initial exacerbation in 1989, I decided to focus even more on the quality of the food I was putting into my body. Eating organic foods of the highest quality became a way of life for me.

Being Your Own Best Advocate

I remember asking one of my first neurologists if there was anything else I could do to help my condition. Even then, I suspected that we were in fact putting chemicals into our bodies every day by way of what we eat and drink. Therefore, it makes sense to pay attention to the food and drink choices we are making.

I had regularly taken vitamins, but after this appointment, I began paying much closer attention to my choices and educating myself on the quality and the ingredients of the foods I was eating. My mother, a nurse practitioner, began extensive research on which supplements were showing promise and if they could possibly help my condition.

With all this new information on which foods I should eat, along with a curated list of helpful supplements, I began my journey into nutrition. I have continued to tweak the foods I eat according to the most current research to insure that I am doing all I can by way of what I put in my body to maximize my health.

One example of this is to make sure my vitamin D levels are significantly higher than average. In fact, under the care of my doctor, I take higher doses of Vitamin D than the FDA recommends. I have done this for years because I have an excellent neuro ophthalmologist who stays up-to-date on studies from around the world and passes these findings along in order help his patients.

My doctor found that people with autoimmune conditions should seek to have higher levels of Vitamin D than those without this particular type of dis-ease. He informed me of the studies that had shown this, and together we decided to increase my levels as the potential benefits for me were extensive. Consequently, I began taking even more of this very inexpensive vitamin for the sake of positive health benefits. Just the same, make sure to consult your own healthcare provider before making any changes to your Vitamin D intake.

During a wonderful (and insightful) phone call I had with my brother some time ago, he spoke of a study that was done on centenarians, those that were living to be one hundred and beyond. The researcher set out to determine what it was that these individuals around the world had in common that allowed them to live well beyond the life expectancy of an average person. After looking into what many would feel were the most obvious factors, such as food, climate, toxins in the environment, genes, etc., they found the one thing all these individuals possessed in surplus was the ability to adapt to the ups and downs of life. They had the ability to be flexible and resilient. The research showed that adaptability is the most important component for life expectancy. Not only does this approach cause life to no longer be a struggle, but it makes our lives so much sweeter and full of happiness. We must always remember that the main purpose of life is to be happy. Ask yourself, "Where do I find joy?"

I began to realize I needed empowerment to find solutions that would allow someone with my complex health to thrive and live a life full of excellence. Being my own best advocate was a lesson I learned early on. Back in 1989, I was told that there was no cure for MS, no treatment to give me hope. In fact, it was difficult to diagnose and oftentimes took several bouts with disabling symptoms or flare-ups for patients to finally receive a diagnosis. While this was extremely frustrating, it gave me the opportunity to take responsibility for *everything* that I was doing to contribute to my health and well-being.

As you can see, there is so much more that you can do for yourself than might be apparent at the beginning. I invite you to keep reading and hope that you continue to be open and curious about learning and applying these choices to your own life. If you choose to take control of your present and your future, I'm certain you will be on your way to greater health and overall well-being.

Listening to Your Body

Managing the Dragon of Fear

66*What you are seeking is not 'out there.' It is within.*99

– Rasha

Anita Moorjani is a woman from Hong Kong who had a magnificent near-death experience. You can read all about it in her fabulous book, *Dying to Be Me*. I had the opportunity to listen to an interview with Anita, and took extensive notes as I knew this information had the power to make a tremendous impact on my life.

I was committed to putting new practices in place and loving myself on a deeper level. My goal has always been healing, stretching from the macro down to the cellular level, and I knew her words could help me facilitate these changes.

The following are my notes and reflections from the interview:

Now that I know who I really am, I will heal.

Anita said, "If you are doing something for another person because you want that person to like you, then you need to ask yourself, 'Is it more important

28

for that person to like me than it is for me to like myself?' In this, I had found the source of one issue I certainly needed to deal with. Unconditionally loving myself and living my life fearlessly should be my top priorities. That hit me right between the eyes! This is exactly what I knew in my heart I needed to do.

You see, loving myself unconditionally was not something that came naturally. I was accustomed to being extremely critical of myself. Similarly, autoimmune dis-eases are where the body attacks itself.

When I realized that this is what I had been doing in my thoughts, and this condition was simply taking that one step further and manifesting itself physically in me, this was indeed an aha moment. I knew it all started with my thoughts, and if I was going to thrive, it started with stopping the self-criticism and learning to love myself unconditionally.

No one is perfect… and I do not need to try to be either!

In addition to the realizations I had in the notes I took, I saw that fear had played such a large role in my life. The unpredictable nature of an autoimmune dis-ease wreaked havoc with those fears: Am I going to wake up one day and painfully lose my vision, as I experienced once before? Is my vision going to be taken from me to the point where I will lose my independence, even to the extreme of not being able to drive a car? Or, worse than any combination of the others, will I no longer be able to take in the beauty of the people I love and the world I live in?

When I look through my left eye only, the damage it sustained now a permanent reality, it scares me that one day my right eye might deteriorate to the same degree. Just like that, my whole world could be like looking through plastic wrap: muted, blurred, distorted depth perception, and ultimately, washed-out. I worried that in a single day, my vibrant world could lose so much of its color. It took me actively living in the present moment to help calm this dragon of fear.

Soon after the second optic-neuritis attack in my left eye, I decided I could no longer handle this constant fear-based thinking. In an effort to conquer these fears, I decided to work at appreciating what I could see *right now* and kept my focus narrowed on that. When those fears came up, I reminded myself to simply appreciate, and would quickly find something beautiful to lock my eyes on. I kept my gaze solely focused on the here and now, leaving the future for tomorrow while I held on to today.

Paying Attention to Our Inner World

A major gift this dis-ease has given me is a high-stakes lecture on how to fully appreciate the little things in life. It has taught me to stop and take the time to really look at all the tiny details of the tremendous beauty inhabiting planet earth. Whether that beauty might take the shape of a single flower, a passing smile, or even the intricacy and complexity of a dedicated ant colony, it is worth appreciating.

We are surrounded by breathtaking beauty and every day gives us a new chance to soak it in. It is a precious practice to me, and I know my physical condition is a direct reflection of my emotional well-being. This parallel is nothing short of astonishing. I have come to see the incredible gravity of being vigilant with what is taking place in my inner world.

There is a song by Rickie Byers-Beckwith titled, *I Am Choosing Heaven Today*. It repeats the truths I have found - we can choose the state that we approach our lives from. It is a choice, and our true power is in how we decide to *respond* to life's joys and challenges.

We can choose the positive road of love, or the negative road of fear. The choice is ours. Go ahead and feel your feelings, but don't be afraid of them. If we take the time to sit and be with our fears, to face them and not run from them, they will melt away.

As we practice facing our fears, we are able to embark on the road to solutions. There is nothing more difficult than standing still, but the decision to move forward will give you freedom to turn from your fears. Try practicing this the next time a fear creeps in. The key here, as my mentor Mary Morrissey says, is to "pay attention to what you are paying attention to." Then, once you know the name of your fears, you can wash them away.

Don't Let Anything Ruin Your Day

I recently purchased a new computer to help me be more efficient with my time and bring this book to completion. After bringing it home and working meticulously to get it all set up properly, I seemed to experience one setback after another. I enlisted the support of store employees, the computer company's training staff, and eventually graduated my way to being helped by troubleshooters at company headquarters; it didn't take long for the whole thing to turn into a circus.

You might think that I was hoping to use the computer for some incredibly technical purposes. Well, that couldn't be much further from the truth! All I wanted was the ability to use my laptop to work on my book project when I was in inspiring locations, such as Florida's stunning Marco Island, and be able to handoff the manuscript when I got home to my desktop. Unfortunately, I was greeted by derailing miscommunication and a flurry of opinions that were rarely consistent. The end result was many wasted hours and the opposite of what I had bought the computer for—efficiency. Add in the frustration I experienced, and you can see that the purchase of the computer looked to be a train wreck.

After hours of fruitless calls, I took a much-needed break to run a few errands. The bank was my last stop before returning home to tackle the project again. Pulling up to the drive-thru window, I was enthusiastically greeted by the teller. As part of her greeting, she asked me how my day had been up to that point. My response, "Well actually, I have had an incredibly challenging day, but I am fine."

She said she was sorry to hear that and asked if I would like a lollipop. A smile instantly stretched across my face and I let out a resounding, "Yes!" Before I drove away, she said something I have tried to always keep in my "emotional tool box," "Keep up the good attitude and never ever let *anything* ruin your day!"

Just like that, the cloud lifted from my day and I drove off with a renewed enthusiasm for the control I had over how I feel in any given moment. I'm pleased to share that it was an absolutely beautiful rest of the day!

While it is a simple story, it provides yet another example of how God places people in our paths to support our journey throughout this life. We just need to recognize them and stop to listen.

Toxic Thinking Creates a Toxic Body

Our thoughts have immense power and, as we now know through scientific advances, that power translates into our bodies. This makes careful monitoring of our thoughts and an awareness of their quality a crucial factor for our optimal health. Supporting this belief, I once heard the following statement, "If you think enough toxic thoughts, your body will become toxic."

We all have the opportunity to work on allowing the energy of our thoughts to be peaceful, joyful, and loving in order to support our health. If there is something or someone who consistently hinders this ability, we need to honor ourselves first and separate from their negativity.

Taking this one step further, it is important to be vigilant in monitoring damaging self-critical thoughts. When I catch my thoughts falling into this pattern, I gently remind myself, "No, that thought left with the multiple sclerosis misdiagnosis."

In order to have a lasting counter to these unhealthy thoughts, try the following. Find an event to tag the thought pattern to. Then, each time it comes up, the reminder allows you to immediately put an end to the sequence and let it go. "No, that thought left with (this event)." Add your own story into the blank and wave goodbye.

The Power of Our Thoughts

You have control. Those are three words that speak to one of the greatest truths about our thoughts. Our thoughts do not have to be something to be afraid of. They can even be an exceptionally useful tool! Take a moment and think about how our inner world ultimately determines the quality of our lives. We have complete control over this aspect of our being. To recognize this is to recognize one of our greatest gifts: our thoughts design what we see and experience in the world.

It is much easier to stay positive and have a healthy outlook when we stay focused on the things we can control. And for the things we can't, we must learn to let them go. In the face of overwhelming challenges, this may sometimes mean something as simple as rising with the intent to shine in the morning. By willing yourself to do something so simple, you have actively decided to not stay in bed all day with the covers pulled over your head. I would call that progress.

Or, as has been proven time and time again, feeling better about ourselves can be a direct result of taking care of the way we look. Engaging in special care with our grooming practices can make a world of difference.

Another important piece of our lives under our control is the organization of our personal space; having a clutter-free environment promotes a clutter-free mind.

There are many simple things that we have control over, even during challenging times. These include slowing down and giving ourselves time to absorb the circumstances, allowing ourselves time to feel those thoughts, taking the time to dissolve whatever fears we might have, and then proceeding with a clear mind.

Calm resolve is the best way I have found to effectively move through even the most challenging of times. The goal is to do so without fear or self-judgment. Ultimately, a clear and calm resolve means keeping one's thoughts focused positively and away from fear and judgment. We are strong, stronger than we know. Allow fear to dissolve and gently remind yourself to move your thoughts toward solutions. Cherish every moment and experience as much peace and joy in each day as possible.

Using A Holistic Approach to Health

66When we participate in our own miracles, the windows of heaven open and fill us with strength.99

– Mary Morrissey

As I am sure you can tell by now, I am on a mission. It has been a serious search for nearly three decades to find ways of bringing more energy into my life, the lives of others and develop methods to sustain that energy for as long as possible. The end goal of this journey is to form a partnership with one's body.

Included in this is developing an awareness of how your body speaks to you, and how it is communicating its needs. For instance, when I overextend my fatigue levels, my body sends me warning signs. These signs leave little room for interpretation. It is almost as if my body is shouting to me, "I need rest." Colossal migraines which demand that I close the shades and lie in bed have been one of the most prominent signs of this fatigue over the years.

Sometimes these situations can last up to three days. I now know at the first sign that I need to make my body the priority. It may be feeling as though I have ignored it, and therefore cries out to me; these clear emergency sirens can't be ignored. In fact, there are times when I need to send in the rescue squad to administer some emergency first-aid!

Another point Anita Moorjani made in her interview was the necessity of realizing our magnificent nature and that we are truly divine. After hearing this, I acted on her suggestion to set up a daily reminder on my phone. There are several phone apps that make it easy to send yourself a message. I now receive a powerful message in the morning and again in the afternoon, which says, "Remember Your Magnificence." Each day I am reminded of this and it is pushed to the front of my thoughts.

Significant change can take place through consistently reminding ourselves of how magnificent we really are. This constant affirmation can help us conquer our denial and save our health.

In her book, *A Return to Love: Reflections on the Principles of a Course in Miracles,* author Marianne Williamson wrote:

"Our deepest fear is not that we are inadequate. Our deepest fear is that we are powerful beyond measure. It is our light, not our darkness that most frightens us. We ask ourselves, 'Who am I to be brilliant, gorgeous, talented, fabulous?' Actually, who are you not to be?

You are a child of God. Your playing small does not serve the world. There is nothing enlightened about shrinking so that other people won't feel insecure around you. We are all meant to shine, as children do. We were born to make manifest the glory of God that is within us.

It's not just in some of us: it's in everyone. And as we let our own light shine, we unconsciously give other people permission to do the same. As we are liberated from our own fear, our presence automatically liberates others."

Powerful Beyond Measure

I see this beautiful quote as being especially significant for those of us facing health challenges and as a key reminder that we are magnificent beyond belief!

Never forget, we are not lessened by our challenges. In fact, we truly are magnificent by living courageously each and every day in the face of whatever those challenges might be. A serious health issue forces us out of our comfort zone to navigate through unfamiliar territory. So yes, we *are* powerful beyond measure.

Clearly, relishing in self-care emboldened by this magnificence has been a significant part of my journey. In fact, it has made a hugely positive impact on both my emotional and physical health.

In the past, holding enough energy had been one of my greatest challenges. This difficulty had an effect on all areas of my life. But, thanks to a change in the way I live, I was able to see that the more I do for myself, the more I end up being able to give to others. Self-care allows me more capacity for love and significantly increased stores of energy.

Experts from all around the world have said that if you are facing a serious illness or have been diagnosed with some alarming condition, it is important to take a look at what has happened in your life in the year or two prior to diagnosis. This time period provides many clues that point to the root of the problem.

In her interview, Anita also touched on the power of resentment. When my marriage ended, I had to look at my situation from 10,000 feet up to see that the resentment I harbored began soon after the start of the marriage. Some early events catapulted my resentment into motion. Feelings of not having control over my life and thoughts of how my partner was negatively impacting me only made the resentment burn hotter. Due in large part to my religious background not supporting divorce, I decided that I needed to honor the choice I had made to marry this man. The resentment only grew.

In hindsight, it is not difficult to point out much of the negativity that exacerbated my illness. I take full responsibility for not making the necessary changes in my life at the time. That being said, I also don't go around beating myself up over it; nothing good comes from that. I know I was doing the best I could at the time with what I knew and with respect to what beliefs I held. What is worthwhile is learning to recognize the clues before they turn into a full-fledged problem. That way, you can continue to grow your energy, your power, your own personal magnificence.

Never Look Back, Keep Moving Forward

Despite the difficulties and the challenges, I am so grateful for everything I have learned and who my journey has led me to become. I am proud of the work I have invested in myself and how that gave me the strength and the courage I needed to leave that difficult relationship. I did so despite what was at stake, because I learned that I am worth it.

You will not see me dwelling on all the years I spent in a devastating marriage, because I choose to thank God that I made the change when I did. I have met the freedom afforded by that decision with a commitment to making the rest of my life the best of my life.

It is important to take an inventory of the relationships we have to see if there are ones that are draining or negative. Get in touch with your inner workings and distance yourself from the toxicity of people who pull you down.

In listening to Anita's interview, I realized that I have a never-ending opportunity when it comes to loving myself. The biggest realization was that I was not loving myself and my life to the level they deserved. I am grateful to have found my passion and know it will bring me to the next level of excellence by feeding my soul. The self-care I learned to give myself allows me to share my OCEANS OF WELLNESS° and my love by helping others conquer their health challenges.

As you will soon find out, I have navigated through challenging times with conventional healthcare providers. In listening to Anita, I could directly relate to her thoughts about conventional medicine when she said, "The energy of conventional medicine can be very fear based."

Using an Open-Minded, Open-Arm Approach

The current medical system places great emphasis on what is wrong, and fails to understand the importance of treating one's self with love and respect. As we have already seen, the toxicity of negative thoughts has the ability to transition from your mind to your body.

Even so, I still believe there is a critical place for conventional medical practices. Emergency situations and where immediate medical intervention or surgery is required need to be treated with respect and understanding. Just because the way a system operates is flawed does not mean that system has nothing worthwhile to offer. With that said, I continue to have a team of conventional healthcare practitioners in place while making sure to choose ones who practice open-mindedness. In addition to the abilities of these professionals, I have an open-arm faith in holistic and integrative medicine, as these approaches take an exceptionally positive approach to our overall health and wellness.

My personal holistic practitioner focuses on my whole being and assists in teaching my body how to be healthy, working all the way down to the cellular level. My doctor told to me early on, "Your cells have forgotten how to be healthy." Knowing this, I must not allow myself to slip back into fear when I am being treated by my conventional doctors. This is critical.

The good news is that many clinics, hospitals, and conventional healthcare practitioners are beginning to see the immense value in complementary and integrative medicine. The blending of all types of healing means the best medicine for us all.

The words of Anita fit in so nicely here; she said that I should look for ways to honor myself. I should stand up for myself and do the things that make me happy and bring me joy, even if that meant laughing at myself. She pointed out that we needed to focus on finding our joy. By doing things that feel great, such as eating foods that make us feel good, we can engage in the love, gentleness, and other positives that are capable of such amazing healing. This was in direct opposition to the many years I felt I was broken and not good enough, ultimately leading to struggles of self-worth.

During the most difficult parts of my life, I did not feel that I was deserving of self-love. Now I see that the NMO was actually my body's way of telling me that my soul was grieving for the loss of its self-worth and identity.

If I had known the truth of who I really was and honored it, I may never have gotten ill in the first place. I have come to know that my emotional feelings were manifesting themselves in my nervous system as illness. This understanding has given me the power to work on healing myself from these patterns of anxiety, fear, and not honoring myself. I am happy to share that I have witnessed my effort's positive and direct effects on my current physical health. I can tell you one thing that is for certain - by taking control of this aspect of my life, I feel incredible!

Finding a Sense of Calm

There is a deep healing that comes from finding peace. When I begin to notice fears creeping in, I simply close my eyes and take three long, deep, cleansing breaths while pouring love into the areas of my body where I can feel the fear. For me, this is usually my chest and solar plexus.

If it is a recurrent fear that I just can't seem to shake, I will close my eyes again and give the fear over to God. I actually see this in my mind as I hand them over to Him. The sense of calm I receive is *always* immediate.

This practice allows me to honor myself while choosing to move through these feelings of fear. The result of washing over this fear with peace shows itself as incredible waves of love. I know this technique to be of huge impact for myself and encourage you to try it as well.

Depending on the level of fear I feel coming on, it may take a few of these sessions to restore my balance, but I know that by pouring love on the fear in this way, I will reap the benefits in return.

Shell 1: The Art and Science of Self-Care

> 66 *The winds of love are blowing all the time. You need only raise your sail to give and receive it.* 99
>
> – Kathryn Ford

What does self-care really mean? To me, it means we take care of ourselves first. It means we practice truly loving ourselves. If we do, we are in far better shape to help everyone else in our lives. Self-care puts us first in line, rather than always telling ourselves, "Well… I will get to 'me' later; right now I have to get this done!"

This is the kind of behavior that eventually landed me in big trouble with my health. My needs would be overlooked and pushed down to the end of the priority list. I realize now that this was backwards. Maybe it doesn't come across as a surprise that this trait seems common to many women, almost as if nurturing is embedded in our DNA.

In order to ensure that I am taking proper care of myself, I now have a wellness routine. Along with putting primarily healthy food, water, and supplements into my body, I have also added additional components that make up my optimally-balanced wellness routine. It has been said before that there are only three things you can control in your life: what you eat, drink, and think. I would add one more thing to this list, and that would be whether you move your body each day. Having a routine is also important, as it helps to ensure that the positive aspects contributing to our overall health and well-being are happening on a regular basis.

Just as it is important to try and take your vitamins and/or medications at the same time each day, doing your very best to never miss a dose, it is consistency in your self-care that makes the real difference over time.

Shell 2: Happy Means Healthy

> 66*Cheerfulness is contagious, but don't wait to catch it from others. Be a carrier!*99
>
> –Unknown

One of my top-three self-care secrets I use to live a life of excellence is to experience happiness each and every day. After all, happy means healthy! But again, Dr. Barbara Fredrickson's research shows that not all things that feel good offer the same benefit on a cellular level. One key way to live "happy means healthy" to the fullest, is to ride the wave of helping or being supportive of someone else. And my favorite Rx to prescribe is that of helping someone else when you are experiencing a challenging time yourself. Not only does it bolster your own positivity (resulting in self-care), but it also creates a more positive and fulfilling life for those that you choose to help.

What does it mean to infuse more joy into my everyday life?

Another one of my daily prescriptions is to infuse joy into my life every single day. I truly believe it goes all the way down to the cellular level and that when we deliberately infuse happiness into our lives, there will be wonderful outcomes that develop on their own. But, we need to be very organized and deliberate to ensure it happens every day. Why? Because our inner pharmacy releases beautiful sparkling healing chemicals that envelop every cell in our bodies when we take part in this consistent joy!

There are studies routinely proving this to be true, and I have seen the effects of seeking joy in my own life. I have even been told that I am the poster child for this truth! When things are not in balance, when the world feels like it is spinning out of control, or if there is something in my life that is toxic, my health takes a turn for the worse. Not just some of the time, but it happens each and every time.

However, when I am deliberate about making sure that I am taking my daily dose of happiness, my body responds in a powerful way. I can actually feel the difference and my health reflects this. And so, I am certain in my belief that a daily prescription of joy needs to be prescribed to all of us for the rest of our lives!

As noted, I make it a choice to be happy every day. The most important job we have is to maximize our happiness, which then supports all other areas of our life, including our health.

Shell 3: Self-Love

To love oneself is the beginning of a lifelong romance.

– Oscar Wilde

As you know, I believe the biggest component of self-care is self-love. That means it is imperative for each of us to direct a deep and profound, pampering love towards ourselves as often as possible.

41

When we do this, it does more for our personal health and well-being than anything else. It is more powerful than any drug or medication. Besides, *it is our birthright to always feel safe, nurtured, loved, and supported.*

We must do whatever we can to bring a daily dose of self-love to ourselves, because 1) it feels so good, and 2) it provides the wonderful side effect of honoring and treating ourselves with more respect and kindness, a vital element of self-care.

Why do flight attendants tell you to put your mask on first?

If there is a drop in cabin pressure, what is the first thing you have been instructed to do? You are told to "place the mask over your face first, and then help others who need assistance" once you have taken care of yourself. For many of us, especially women, this sort of "me first" behavior seems unnatural and maybe even comes across as selfish. Many of us are conditioned to put our needs at the bottom of a very long list of priorities that include our children, spouse, boss, co-workers, friends, and family.

We have got to take care of ourselves first, because that is when we are capable of being our best for everyone else around us. For many years, I did not understand this truth. On a cognitive level I understood, but I certainly did not practice it. I was still trying to skirt the issue and make sure everything else was taken care of first.

But, more often than not, there wasn't much leftover to give myself. I realize now I had it backwards. I now know how vitally important it is for my well-being to ensure that I am taken care of. Unfortunately for me, it took a major illness to knock some sense into my head and heart. It is my hope that you will be able to prevent something similar from happening to you.

So, the question is begging to be asked, what turned the corner for my health? Unfortunately, I let things get so bad that there was no choice but to make 'me' the priority; my life was at stake. I am not neglectful with others, but I certainly was with myself.

I have needed to practice treating "me" with respect and being as loving with myself as I am with others. How I treat other people is how I must also treat myself. It hasn't always been easy, but the result has been taking my life back.

As mentioned before, this is a journey into healing your body through self-care and self-love. But, even so, we still tend to help, help, help first, and then think about our own needs last. As I already stated, perhaps we have it backwards. At the end of the day, maybe this is why we find ourselves out of balance and physically drained. I am instead suggesting that we flip this mindset around to make self-care and self-love our top priority.

Shell 4: Relentless Pampering

> ❝We must honor what it is that indulges or gratifies each of our own personal desires. Then, allow those delicious feelings to wash over every cell in our body.❞
>
> – Kathryn Ford

I am a firm believer in relentless pampering! It just sounds so amazing, doesn't it? In order to understand all of the benefits that pampering can bring, we need to explore this practice and what it means to our body, mind, and spirit.

As defined by Princeton's WordNet, pampering is "the act of indulging or gratifying a desire." I have to admit; I love that description because I feel it most closely defines what pampering really means to me.

The true definition of pampering is unique to each of us. We must honor that which indulges or gratifies our own personal desires and make that wanting a reality. The real beauty of this is that *you* get to decide what being pampered means to you.

I discovered early on that connecting with nature is at the top of my list for feeling pampered. So, every morning when I take my little dog, Teddy, for a walk, I get in touch with nature. I do this by listening to the doves coo, or I may take a peak at the dolphins swimming in the ocean and soak in the beauty of nature waking up all around me. By doing this, I am allowing the sparkling, magnificent feelings I receive to wash over every cell in my body.

What if I don't have the extra money to spend on myself?

An important point to make on the subject of pampering is that it doesn't need to be expensive. It must, however, be connected to what feeds your spirit. For instance, I love sunset walks on the beach and I am blessed to live at the beach in Santa Monica, California. There is something so very powerful about the sand and the combination of the rays of the sun at either sunrise or sunset. To me, that is truly divine. So for my interests, my daily gift of pampering doesn't cost anything at all. On the other side of the spectrum, I also absolutely love a long weekend at a resort spa up in the mountains, my favorite being the Sanctuary at Camelback Mountain. What I want to make clear is that it does not need to cost you anything to give yourself the gift of pampering. But if you can and have the desire, certainly go for it and splurge a little… or a lot!

Again, we must honor what it is that indulges or gratifies each of our own personal desires. We must wash ourselves with whatever it is that makes our heart sing physically, emotionally, and spiritually.

Grains of Sand

Be Well! Exercise #1: is to set aside 15-20 minutes and think about what *LOVE* means to you by answering the following questions:

* How do you express love towards yourself?
* What is one new way you would enjoy expressing love?
* How does it feel when you receive self-love?
* Where do you notice this expression of love show up in your body?

It is important that we get in tune with our body and the messages it sends us. For example, mine shows up in the feeling of my heart expanding. I have noticed that I tend to put my hand on my heart while my chest fills with this overwhelming love. Learning how to notice when your body speaks is critical. I believe that imbalance in our health is often due to an ignoring of messages from our bodies.

Not long ago, I was sharing something with my coach and mentor, Mary Morrissey, about a particularly stressful situation I was working through. Her first words of advice for me were to pay attention to my body and any signals or communications it was sending. She reminded me of the importance of this practice when she said, "Kathryn, you have already demonstrated that you have the capacity to ignore messages from your body."

If I am going to be honest with myself, I had various signs surface a full two years prior to my diagnosis. However, I chose to not take care of myself emotionally, which—in my belief—led to my subsequent diagnosis.

Dr. Bernie Siegel, who wrote the foreword to this book, has written on the relationship between the patient and the healing process. "If I told patients to raise their blood levels of immune globulins or killer T cells, no one would know how. But, if I can teach them to love themselves and others fully, the same change happens automatically. The truth is: Love heals." Understanding the importance of his words, the life-dependent need for love that we all have, we can realize the necessity to engage in a routine of self-love. We can remind ourselves on a daily basis that we are magnificent and deserving of a beautiful and healthy life.

Be Well! Exercise #2: is to set aside 15-20 minutes to examine the following:

* What is your body, mind, and spirit calling for in the way of pampering?

Once you have come to your own answer, commit to and schedule one new pampering activity to indulge in this week.

Our Journey Is Underway

It has been a true pleasure to be able to share these practices with you. I invite you make the time to practice the tips and tools given to you so far. At the very least, I hope you start pampering yourself a bit more often. After all, who wouldn't want more of that? Well, perhaps you just needed a little nudge, so I am officially giving you a prescription for pampering and self-love!

GRATITUDE

Gratitude allows for healing from the inside out, and a consistent dose brings about incredible results. It is the open door to abundance in all areas of our lives, and is especially effective in healing our physical bodies. So, how does one get these amazing benefits? By being grateful! It is as simple as that. By moving away from negative emotional patterns, we can see the immense benefits in our health and overall well-being. The power of gratitude is evidenced in miraculous healings that otherwise have no explanation. Scientific research has shown that expressions of gratitude can massively improve our immune systems. So, let's explore how we can incorporate this amazing medicine into our daily lives!

Healing from The Inside Out

In This Chapter

* Surrendering to the good, even in the face of challenges
* Finding blessings and healing forces in order to thrive

> 66At any one time, our health is the sum total of
> all the impulses, positive and negative, emanating
> from your consciousness.99
>
> – Deepak Chopra

Gratitude opens the door to abundance in every area of our lives, including our health and well-being. In this chapter, we will dive deep into the immense power of gratitude. You can trust me when I say that embracing gratitude has been the most important practice for me in recent years. When I express deep and profound gratitude, life works so beautifully. I have set an intention to be grateful for all things, letting it bring close the good and spill over to transform the bad.

Practicing a life of gratitude has helped with my own stress levels during challenging times, which in the past would have launched me into a state of high anxiety. Now, I am able to quickly shift over to asking myself, "What are the gifts in this situation?" By focusing on the positive, my personal perspective changes and my inner world magically transforms; I am able to recognize the fact that it is me who is responsible for the world I create and choose to live in.

Gratitude: The Free Wonder Drug!

It is a miracle when we finally realize and come to see that gratitude is the open door to abundance. This abundance takes a host of different forms, not limited only to my health, but spanning to all areas of my life! The more of this goodness that I allow to flow through to me, the more gratitude and abundance I can pass along to my clients and the other people in my life. It doesn't take long for gratitude to expand and bring us to a life of full-spectrum wealth. It is such a fulfilling way to live when we are experiencing abundance in all areas of our lives, including our health, relationships, and freedom of time and money! One of the most stunning benefits of a life of abundance just happens to be the ability to maintain your youthfulness!

Gratitude is an absolute necessity for comprehensive well-being. It is as important as taking a medicine or required prescription every day. I can 100% say that I will be "on" gratitude for the rest of my life; the profound results I have experienced have shown me the precious and liberating power that it brings.

Focusing on the positive things in our lives, instead of those aspects that might not be so great, allows gratitude to work as the most powerful (and inexpensive) wonder drug on the market. Bathing each day in appreciation is a fun and magical way to live!

Arianna Huffington spoke of the two years of hard work she put in to get her online blog, the Huffington Post, up and running. She worked tirelessly for her success, almost to the point of total burnout. One day in her office, she passed out because she was so overworked and was failing to take care of herself. She fell and hit her face on her desk, breaking her cheekbone and cutting her eye. This was her wakeup call, her body pleading with her to understand that she was burned out and working far too much. In that moment, she realized that she did not have a balanced life. This was a turning point for her. Today, Ariana lives a more balanced life and advocates that it is clearly more fun to live this way. This is what life is all about.

I know now that what we focus on tends to be the very same thing that we get the most of, so focusing on the good things in life is sure to bring more our way. As I said before, practicing gratitude is something I will do for the rest of my life because the side effects are just so amazing. Besides, the doctor ordered it!

When my inner physician told me that it was in my best interest to realize the importance of and practice daily gratitude, I knew I had to listen. This is one medicine where the list of negative side effects is nonexistent and the rewards are unending!

Living with Health Challenges

Over the past three decades, I have lived with the diagnosis of a serious autoimmune dis-ease that, looking back, has been both my greatest challenge and one of my greatest gifts. Of course, I would never wish this upon anyone else, but I know that the journey I have been on has transformed me into the person I am today. For that I am eternally grateful.

In the Face of Darkness

Surrender to A Higher Power

"Not until we are lost do we begin to understand ourselves."

–Henry David Thoreau

The greatest challenge I have experienced with my diagnosis is the accompaniment of severe, chronic fatigue. I live with the kind of fatigue that feels like no amount of sleep could ever make the exhaustion go away. It is a bone-numbing tiredness, one that persists throughout the day with severity levels that often feel as if I have hit a wall. At that point, all I can do is collapse onto my bed. The challenge with this level of fatigue is that it affects every aspect of my life. When it strikes, there is simply no escaping it.

However, even with this severe NMO-induced exhaustion, I have discovered that the real quality of my life depends entirely on me being able to participate in the things that bring me joy. Sometimes this is easier said than done, but it is true just the same.

I firmly believe it is possible to have a serious health challenge *and still live a life of excellence.* This belief is at the heart of my life, and hear me when I say that it is possible! I invite you to embrace this understanding, allowing it to give you and your loved ones a sense of empowerment.

More Than Meets the Eye

Many people who know me have said the following at one point or another: "Wow, it is hard to believe that anything is wrong. You look so good. You look so healthy." While I am thankful for these affirmations, they can cause us to overlook the challenges I have been through.

Like many people with an autoimmune condition, the challenges and the struggles I have faced remain largely invisible. There was even a point where I was so tired of being sick that I could scream. I rarely talked about the details of my illness during the nearly three decades I lived with it. You might ask me, "Kathryn, why is that?" Well, mainly because I would rather turn my focus to things that bring me joy. Not only that, but I am a private person by nature. These pages clearly show that I have had to overcome many roadblocks in order to share my personal life with the rest of the world.

I have faced the trials with the help of my angels. Doreen Virtue, an author I greatly respect, taught me that those same angels are waiting and ready to help us. All we need to do is ask. And, ask I did!

The following excerpt is from Neale Donald Walsch's book, *When Everything Changes, Change Everything*: "Knowing that all things turn out for the best, that all outcomes are perfect for your evolution, gives you extraordinary confidence in tomorrow. And that's where your power lies." Now, when situations appear in my life that I don't understand, or ones come about that seem extremely challenging or dark, I write them down and put them in a special folder that says, "It Will Be Revealed in Time If It Needs to Be."

By doing this, I find it easier to remember that I truly believe that everything happens for a reason, and a very good one at that! I do believe, as I tell myself and others regularly, that there is a gift in every situation. By using my folder, I can strive to be mentally patient for the gift to reveal itself while I remember to express gratitude in all things.

Initially, I choose to focus on the fact that there is at least one gift in every challenging situation, even if it may not be fully revealed from the start. This allows me to express gratitude for every situation even in the face of difficulty. In addition, I immediately write down all my blessings, taking special note of the people and things in my life that I am grateful for.

It is by focusing on this gratitude that we can transform our situation from a harsh pain to a softness that brings peace and calm into our lives, even when obstacles are present. Our emphasis on gratitude leads us from focusing on the problem to asking ourselves what is trying to emerge in our lives. We only need to let go of old patterns in order to proceed toward freedom and peace, leading us to living a larger life than we could have ever dreamed to be possible.

I feel this quote from an unknown author sums my thoughts up best, "The sun is always shining, we need only remove the clouds." Similarly, as Derek Rydell says, "A problem is solved when we evolve."

From the Inside Out

I believe the NMO is my body's way of responding to psychological traumas in my life which, to a certain degree, I chose to bury instead of work through. This dis-ease has certainly been a wake-up call and I say that in the most positive way possible. It has prompted me to change the way I live, how I structure my thoughts, and to heal from the inside out. My health challenges provided me with insight to my inner self, helping me find understanding of my own inner resources.

This propelled me on my soul's journey like nothing else could have. Similarly, it brought me to a level of compassion and caring for others that no other experience had. A plummet in my health carried me to a place of knowing God and trusting that everything that happens to us is a gift, one that nourishes our souls.

I have truly arrived at a place where I can finally "let go and let

God." This has been said many times before and in many different ways, but here are two of my personal favorites: "What you resist persists" and "Everything changes with a change in point of view."

We all go through vistas and valleys, challenges and breakthroughs in life, and each of these experiences help us to understand the experiences of others. I am grateful for this vantage point and for the gift of being able to deeply and intimately understand what others are going through.

When we are sad and scared (feelings which often accompany health challenges), we cut ourselves off and feelings of darkness and isolation prevail. Too often, in this state, we start to believe that we are left out in life. During the dark times we face, we tend to isolate ourselves, continuing a vicious cycle that keeps us in that dark place instead of facing it head-on and moving through it. Be aware when self-isolation has taken over, and don't go through the challenging times alone. By bringing in another person, you connect with your own inner being and can better work through any situation.

Almost all change produces fear on some level. When you feel that fear, ask yourself, "What needs my loving attention right now?" In most cases, and in the face of a health challenge, it is YOU needing your loving attention. Joy in one's life is nature's best prescription for health. As Dr. Albert Schweitzer, the great physician and philosopher once said, "Each person carries his own doctor inside him. We are at our best when we give the doctor who resides within each patient a chance to go to work." Wise words indeed.

A Shift in Perception

With respect to the challenge of NMO fatigue, routine is extremely important for balancing and managing this condition. A long time ago, I realized that I would need to plan ahead when something important was coming up that I wanted to do. I did this by "banking" energy. I would rest for a day or two before the important event, and I also planned to recover and rejuvenate for a day or two afterwards.

Even though it sounds like a great deal of planning, the benefits have absolutely been worth it. I have found that it is enormously important to the quality of my life and ultimately, my overall well-being. I have made the decision that all of the should-do tasks will not always be accomplished by me. If it is not a necessity in life, or does not bring me joy, I simply cannot spend the finite amount of energy I have on it.

Since I am a perfectionist by nature, I needed to get my priorities straight very early on, and I am so very thankful for the amazing people in my life who have supported me and understood my situation. They are the ones who have ultimately picked up a great deal of extra on my behalf. All of this has made an incredible difference in my day-to-day living.

The strong bonds created, and feelings of love that radiate from these sometimes tricky situations, are filled with the vibration of love, which is—of course—the most powerful vibration in the universe.

The biggest challenge I had to overcome in order to embrace my challenges was to allow others to provide me with help and support. I was the type of person who wanted to be superwoman, like my mom, but I knew that I needed to let go of the guilt and shame I was hanging onto for not being able to do it all. Yes, in the beginning, I felt less valuable than others in my family because I simply could not live up to the standard I had set for myself. So I needed to shift my perception and return the feeling of value to myself. This allowed the love to pour in, and a huge weight was lifted from my shoulders.

In hindsight, I can see how I was imposing these terrible feelings upon myself. I needed to let go of the life I had always dreamed of and embrace the one that was waiting for me. While a health challenge can certainly upset expectations and disrupt dreams, it does not need to destroy them.

Learning strategies for managing these changes can help to promote new understandings of loss, and this in turn can help us move forward. After allowing ourselves to grieve a specific loss, we can then take a look at the bright side and the many blessings we each have. This will lead us to *looking forward* to our future, one that includes our most stunning dreams.

54

It is common for someone who has been diagnosed with a serious medical condition to feel as if their life is over and their dreams have been shattered. Believe me, I know this feeling. When you are faced with challenges that seem completely out of your control, it can be stressful and scary to the point that your world might seem saturated with doom and gloom.

However, I am here to tell you that there is another path to follow. A path filled with light and dreams and vitality. While the specific definitions may change, they are available to all of us. I am not saying it is always easy to be optimistic, especially as my own optimism has been tested many times along the way. But I promise you this - if you can shift into and ultimately find your optimism, which comes after taking sufficient time to integrate and grieve, it will be worth its weight in gold. You are well worth the effort it takes!

Surrender to What Is, Then Continue to Live

In most instances, you can't change your diagnosis, but you can modify what it does to you. I have found that there is a beautiful sweetness when I am able to let go of what my life was and surrender to a higher power. It is in that moment that my life is no longer a struggle and it begins to get easier.

Even though it might not seem to be true, you have control; you get to choose how to manage your challenges. I pray to a higher power, one that I refer to as God, and encourage others to follow whatever their spiritual path might be. It is not my intention to get caught up in the name we give this power, but to ensure that we are comfortable relating to it. That is what really matters.

As mentioned before, I now know that my purpose in life is to share what I have learned along my journey and to help others who are facing their own health challenges. It is my life's work to help them successfully navigate their own journeys.

Meditation and prayer are two of the many tools that I will be presenting, and they are just two of the very powerful practices that will bring you to a place of living a life of excellence.

I am humbled that you have decided to come along on this journey to OCEANS OF WELLNESS® with me. I am deeply and profoundly grateful that our journeys are now entwined. Thank you!

It is my wish to bless you fully with the knowledge of the ocean of possibilities within each of us and to show you how to take a deep dive in order to access it.

Finding The Good in A Challenging Situation

❝Expectancy is the atmosphere for miracles.❞

– Edwin Louis Cole

My life as a young adult began with dreams and hopes of a full and fabulous life. As a twenty-two year old college graduate, and a newly-engaged young woman, I had the opportunity to relocate from Minnesota to Oklahoma City to begin my new career with a national corporation.

Prior to graduating, this company had made me an offer that I simply could not refuse; that, to be honest, was the most exciting part of it all! The scary part was that I needed to relocate to Oklahoma, a move that would prove to be quite the adventure.

My fiancé and I settled into an adorable townhome in the northwest part of Oklahoma City. The property featured fantastic amenities, like a gated entrance, an expansive swimming pool, and gorgeous, modern surroundings. The area was new, beautiful, and—best of all—affordable, notably important since the economy of Oklahoma at the time was severely depressed due to the state of the oil industry.

This was an early lesson in some of the good that may present itself in a negative situation; it just requires that you recognize it and position yourself to take advantage of it. My salary, company car, and great benefits package allowed me and my fiancé to live the good life. We had strong hopes that he would land a great job as well, as he had previously earned a Master of Business Administration/MBA.

The Honeymoon is Over, Time for Plan B

Our new life seemed to be going as perfectly as planned. Eventually, my fiancé found a job as a director at a private elementary school in the city, which he really seemed to enjoy. We had an absolutely magical wedding back in Minnesota and I thought to myself that this was everything I had ever wanted. But one short month later, my brand new husband lost his job.

This would prove to be a defining moment for us, as the first year of our marriage turned out to be nothing short of a disaster. He began searching for work, but besides some part-time teaching at a local college, the months dragged on without success.

After many agonizing discussions, we decided that he should go back to Minnesota, live with my parents temporarily, and look for a job there. Our plan was that once he found a job, I would join him and begin searching for a new position. It was a difficult decision, but one we felt we needed to make, so we set it into action.

Fast forward a few weeks and his move was finished, putting over 700 miles between us; clearly this was not an ideal way for us to enjoy our first year of marriage together. But that was our story for the time being - I was living in Oklahoma and he was living with my parents in Minnesota. It was emotionally draining to be the sole breadwinner, living in a new city where I knew very few people, and I didn't really have the time to establish lasting friendships. Simply stated, I was twenty-three years old and I felt completely isolated and alone.

To make matters even more challenging, this was at a time where it was incredibly expensive to call home. I am sure that we can all remember a time not so long ago when long-distance charges were a very real thing. My mother was cooking, cleaning, and doing my husband's laundry. At the same time, he was using my father's car for transportation.

Even though my parents are extremely giving and generous people, I knew they had to be wondering *why* he was unable to find employment as the months dragged on. For the type of position he was seeking at the time, it was unusual for the search to be so fruitless. Even now, so many years later, I can recall the distinct feeling that my life was spinning out of control. To say I was drowning in stress would be an understatement.

A Second Chance Opportunity

It was now May of 1987, and my husband had spent almost five months looking for employment in Minnesota with no success. It was starting to dawn on me that I needed to take matters into my own hands if I was going to get us out of this frustrating situation.

The next step I took was to put out some feelers regarding open positions back in Minnesota. Fortunately, things were lining up. I became aware of a great position with a cosmetics company and applied immediately.

I had worked as a sales consultant for this same company at a major department store while I was in college, and I knew that I would enjoy the job. It was for an account coordinator position, which required traveling to their different stores to support and train the consultants working behind the counter; after reading this far, you can see why I knew that this position was a perfect fit!

After an initial phone interview, I was granted one of the final interview spots for meeting in person. I immediately flew to Minnesota to give it all that I had. There was a tremendous amount of competition for the job and I knew that I needed to be at my best to land it. And land it I did! Thankfully, that was the end result for this story. However, in the moments between flying out and finally accepting the position, there would be unwanted times of intense worry and drama.

As Fate Would Have It...

My parents lived about an hour and twenty minutes from downtown Minneapolis, where the interview was to take place. The initial plan was for my husband to drive me to the interview, allowing me to give my complete and total focus to the big day I had ahead of me.

The day before, however, we had a huge argument when he realized that he had scheduled an informational coffee interview for the same morning as my interview in Minneapolis. I asked him to reschedule, as I did not want to feel rushed. He refused, but promised to be home in time to get me to the interview with plenty of time to spare.

When the time came that we should have been leaving, he was nowhere to be found. As this was the only vehicle we had to get to the interview, I went into an absolute state of panic when it became clear that I was going to be late. There was no way to reach him, as this was before cell phones, and he made no attempt to let me know what was going on.

Finally, with only an hour left before my appointment, he arrived back at my parent's home. I was livid and cried with frustration all the way to Minneapolis; I could not understand how he could do this to us.

By this point, he had been job hunting for nearly seven months and was unable to receive even one offer. I had a chance at getting us out of our tumultuous situation, and my husband nearly sabotaged it.

Needless to say, I did not get to have the calm, centering time in advance of my interview that I had hoped for. However, I asked for God's help in letting my stressful morning fade into the background, and with an answered prayer, I did very well in the various meetings with all of the high-level executives. But you already know the answer to that—I got the job!

Given the chaos of the morning, the fact that they hired me felt like a full-blown miracle. I was thrilled! But, as I would later realize, this was just one of many moments that would impact my health and well-being.

With my new position secured, we immediately began planning our move back home to Minnesota. I resigned from the position I held in Oklahoma City, and before I knew it, we were on our way back up north in a small U-Haul truck filled with our belongings. After running out of gas in the middle of nowhere, and a few other unexpected adventures along the way, we made it back to Minnesota. I could finally breath again.

Looking back, one lesson I wish I had learned from all of this was to reach out and ask for help. Being a very private person, I felt as though I was being a burden to others by sharing my worries, my concerns, and ultimately, my problems. I had allowed my husband living at my family's home to be a huge source of stress for me. I knew my parents would do anything for me and wanted to help, but I also knew that the situation was filling their lives with discomfort; for that, I was terribly sorry.

Shortly after our move back to Minnesota, my husband was able to get an entry-level position with a large publishing company in their telemarketing department. It was a small start, but we had hopes that he could advance with the company once he had gotten his foot in the door.

Our first anniversary arrived, and I am pleased to say that we were both employed and still alive. I considered that a huge feat. At this point, we had very little money with the expenses of air travel, the move, and trying to make it on one salary. So, with little to pad the bank, we decided to live in a neighborhood in South Minneapolis and be the caretakers of a small apartment building in order to reduce our rent.

However, our plan to save money came with a price tag of its own. We found that where we lived was only contributing to our stress, and the situation peaked when a murder took place in the alley across from our apartment. The stress grew, but we stuck to our master plan of aggressively saving to someday soon purchase our own home. About a year-and-a-half later, just in the nick of time, we were in a position to make that purchase.

I did not realize it at the time, but my first "dark night of the soul" was unfolding and would culminate in a health crisis in May of 1989; I was about to completely lose the sight in my left eye. I never thought something so devastating and horrific could happen to me. It would slightly improve over time, but since those terrifying days when the stabbing pain persisted, what I see when using that eye can only be described as looking through plastic wrap.

Even though we had purchased a new home together, there were challenges with our marriage. Trust issues began to set in. Deceit began to appear in the form of lies, secrets, and not sharing important information that affected me and my health. Unknown to me, our insurance company had threatened to cancel our coverage due to a road rage incident my husband had been involved in. We were being sued and I had no clue!

Then there were the financial indiscretions that kept me constantly off balance. Sometimes it felt like the stream of problems were unending. All of this took its toll and I know now that by not effectively dealing with these issues, they became extremely detrimental to my health and well-being.

What I did not do was find my own voice in my marriage. Honestly, this was primarily because I felt like I didn't have one. Those are the feelings that were trapped inside of me that would eventually lead to an overall feeling of resentment. My emotional energy was drained, and I felt my world spiraling out of control.

As modern dance pioneer Martha Graham once said, "The body never lies—it says what words cannot." My body was screaming for me to wake up. It wanted me to notice what was happening and to take the necessary actions required to stop the turmoil. It wanted me to put an end to the struggle of not knowing what terrible thing was going to happen next.

My body wanted me to find my authentic self, one that is filled with joy. However, since I wasn't listening to my body's gentle nudging's, it decided to start a battle.

Unexpected Blessings

Allow The Dis-ease to Heal Your Life

❝People who learn to control inner experience will be able to determine the quality of their lives, which is as close as any of us can come to being happy.**❞**

- Mihaly Csikszentmihalyi

In Dr. Bernie Siegel's book, *Peace, Love & Healing*, he reveals the following truths: "True healers know the value of afflictions and of adversity. They know that within the symbolic experience of dis-ease lies a path to change and self-healing and a healthy bodymind. Let us start on that path. Allow the dis-ease to heal your life. Begin your journey and become your authentic self, now."

When I first read these words so many years ago, I felt as if his message had been handcrafted for me. It was one of life's grand coincidences in play. My mother once had the pleasure of listening to Dr. Siegel speak and received a signed copy of his life-changing book. Many years later, I was perusing the shelves of my parent's library for something to help me pass the time.

And there it was, just waiting for me to take it off the shelf and uncover the truths inside. As I am sure you can imagine, I was thrilled to find a book so well-aligned with my journey; it fit perfectly into that magical time and place where I could understand and relate to what was being said!

As I skimmed the pages to get a general feel for what I was about to read, I saw a quote that would change my life: "Accepting our mortality as a motivator and not denying it, looking into the shadows of our unconscious, developing self-love and self-esteem—this is what I want to share with you. As a surgeon I know incredible things can happen when energy is freed for healing. We are looking beyond quantity (the province of medicine) to quality of life."

Not much later, I would find another quote that resonated with me, one that gave me hope and backed up the powerful truth that had gripped me: "Still, there is no denying that not every physical illness can be cured. We can, however, make use of all illness to help us redirect our lives."

In that moment, as I stood in my parent's library reflecting on my life, I knew that my body was asking me to adjust my course. It was asking me to redirect my focus to one of unrivaled joy, peace, and love.

Standing with Dr. Bernie Siegel's book in hand, I began to think about my own achievements in life. What was clear to me was that the greatest accomplishment in my life, more than any other thing I had done, was bringing my son Andrew into this world. I am eternally grateful for the stunning waves of joy, peace, and love I have had the privilege of experiencing with, and because of, him.

I am so proud of the amazing young man he has grown up to be, and he truly is my pride and joy. As I have said thousands of times to him (and expect to say thousands more), "I am the luckiest mom in the whole wide-world to have the most wonderful son in the whole wide-world!"

Through all the challenging and dark times on my journey, Andrew's zest for life and bright light have illuminated the way. Even as a little boy, his light had the ability to shine right through any challenge. He has always been my greatest gift, and I love him beyond words. He has provided true joy for me through the darkest of times. He has provided a degree of balance for me along the roughest roads.

Redirecting One's Focus

Like many others, I believe that a dis-ease is a manifestation of unbalanced energy. To paint a picture of the damaging effects of an unbalanced life, let's go back to my early adulthood, specifically my newlywed days.

In hindsight, it is easy to see how my extreme feelings of frustration resulted in a crescendo of toxic energy. Seemingly out of the blue, I was stunned by the diagnosis that I had multiple sclerosis. I wish now, in looking back at my early life, that I would have recognized the effect of my toxic stress and how it had played such a powerful role in my diagnosis. Knowing then what I know now, I could have made better decisions that were more balanced for my health and well-being.

But that's not my story, and I am grateful for that. I was given a second chance to experience this precious life by uncovering and making more balanced decisions for my health and well-being. The most devastating news in my life would turn out to be a gift; is there any better example of finding light in a dark space? And that, my dear friend, can be your story as well.

A health challenge is just that—a challenge. It is a chance for you to rise up and achieve something incredible. Finding positivity in the midst of trials brings about the kind of story we all want to hear. So, here are just a few of the positive aspects a health challenge can bring forth. They come in the form of a list I made of the things I hold dearest and closest to my heart:

* My faith
* My amazing son, Andrew
* My parents and family
* My friends
* My strength
* My little dog, Teddy
* And, finally having an accurate diagnosis

For me, success has come from balancing hope and realism. A serious illness can be an extremely lonely journey, and oftentimes people do not know what to say when we break the news to them. It can be difficult for others to fathom that the best medicine is often for them to just be there for us. No words, no attempts to fix what is broken, just to be there.

In the animal kingdom, when danger hovers over a group of monkeys, they instinctively huddle together and groom each other feverishly. While this does not remove the danger, it does reduce the anxiety and loneliness of the situation.

This need for support is not only present when we find our doctors breaking terrible news to us, but continues as we are faced with *managing* our diagnosis. Talk with your loved ones and let them know that the most important thing they can do for you is to simply spend time with you and let you know that you are not alone.

When a friend was diagnosed with breast cancer several years ago, I asked if there was anything I could do for her. She made a request that, on several mornings, right after she arrived home from the hospital, I would swing by Starbucks for coffee and then bring it to share with her. It was a simple, yet profound, request.

The Presence of Love and Support

It was with great pleasure that I had the privilege of joining her for coffee upstairs in her bedroom on those first mornings after her surgery. Sometimes we sat in silence with the TV on in the background. Other times, we chatted up a storm, taking great delight in telling each other about our children. We even talked about her fears and sometimes I simply rubbed her back. I was there for her and I did not need to say or do anything special. All she wanted was my presence, love, and support.

Dr. Bernie Siegel states, in reference to changing the body by changing the mind, "What the placebo suggests to us is that we may be able to change what takes place in our bodies by changing our state of mind. Therefore, when we experience mind-altering processes - for example, meditation, hypnosis, visualization, psychotherapy, love and peace of mind—we open ourselves to the possibility of change and healing."

Dis-ease has been my teacher. While this may sound strange at first, once I looked beyond the surface of my condition, it became readily apparent that there was so much I had learned from the challenges to my personal life and to my health. In fact, the biggest lesson it taught me was to love myself unconditionally. The feelings associated with this new and amazing concept were the exact opposite of the self-criticism I had been so accustomed to in the past.

There are many other concepts I have learned from these health challenges, either directly or indirectly, and mostly they relate to the idea of self-love. Fortunately for me, one expression of self-love was changing my perception of the health challenges in my life and using them for healing.

The words of Dr. Bernie Siegel confirmed what I already knew and had experienced within my own life—opening ourselves to self-love can have an enormous impact on our bodies. My dis-ease has taught me all of this and so much more!

Possibilities of Change and Healing

I have had phenomenal miracles result from my mental yoga practice. I have tailored it to include visualizing, affirmations, meditation, and an ever-present positive approach to whatever is happening in my life. I find the truth of what I want, see myself as already having it, and then I hold this vision in my mind.

If I see that I have unconsciously let my focus slip onto my condition, I gently press my internal "pause button" and bring my thoughts right back to whatever it might be that I would love to experience.

Several years back, I had an MRI that showed a lesion on my brain stem. Needless to say, that is a frightening thing for anyone to be informed of! After an extended length of time had passed, another MRI was ordered. Guess what they found? The lesion was no longer there!

Was that a miracle? Absolutely it was. But, I also attribute this change to holding the vision of getting better with each passing day; every day, I would "see" myself as being in perfect health. There is nothing like a miracle to light a fire and inspire you to live a life of excellence!

Your Shortcut to Thriving

66*Experience is not what happens to a person; it is what a person does with what happens to them.*99

–Aldous Huxley

In many ways, the dis-ease has changed my life for the better, often in ways that I never could have imagined. As mentioned before, I see now that my health challenges have been a powerful gift. I have dug deep to move beyond limiting health issues and uncover that truly loving myself is the key.

This learning process has also taught me that the more I love myself, the more I feel love overflowing from me out to others. As I pour love into myself, it creates a ripple that touches many of the people in my life. I now have more love to give than ever before!

By embodying the change that I wish to see, living from my heart and that place of authenticity, the series of discoveries along the way have been nothing short of breathtaking! My personal outcome has lead to a more conscious, steadily balanced, and strikingly beautiful life.

In addition to loving myself first and seeing that love expand to encompass others, four stepping stones have emerged from this unconditional love. One could even call them the "four cornerstones to healing."

The Four Stepping Stones of My Healing Journey

1. **Stand Up for Yourself** - By strengthening our boundaries, we accept one of the most powerful ways to honor ourselves and step out of the need many of us have to be "people pleasers." When we speak our truth, we feel more confident, freeing us to say what we feel and to ask for what we want.

On the other hand, weak boundaries allow the opinions of others to determine our self-worth, which has the potential to be extremely destructive to our well-being. I can now see that I had taken on the job of criticizing myself, just as others had criticized me. When we do this, we are operating from a position of fear rather than one of love. This is in direct opposition to expressing our true feelings, which inevitably lead to a healthy state of mind that filters down into our bodies.

As you strengthen your boundaries, you will increase your self-confidence and naturally begin to feel the power of self-respect. I spent much of my life feeling inferior. I frequently set aside my own feelings and happiness in order to let others shine. In fact, experiencing the challenge of a chronic condition only made matters worse for me. After I was no longer able to continue working, I remember telling a close friend that I felt broken… broken and not as worthy as other people.

While those were my feelings back then, I am now better equipped to allow myself to be who I really am. I have made the conscious decision to use my personal health journey as a catalyst for living an exceptional life. I chose to look at my situation as an opportunity for change and that began with honoring myself first. It didn't happen overnight, but one piece at a time has led to an assembled whole. I now know that despite my health challenges, I am a magnificent person living the best version of my life! I am standing in the power of who I truly am. I am remembering and yielding to my magnificence as Rev. Michael Beckwith proclaims we all should do.

As alluded to before, this dis-ease was partially a byproduct of fear. That emotion subtly began to affect the cells of my body. My decisions were not bringing me joy, as I was making them out of fear. Living in the now or in the present moment has helped me create my future from a place of peace and calm. I have found that maximizing my emotional state directly contributes to my well-being.

The greatest realization I gleaned from my battles with fear is that we are meant to be happy, truly and entirely happy. In order to ensure this is my reality, I am constantly performing quick checks to confirm that each and every decision I make is founded in love and joy.

2. **Finding Your Voice** - Letting others know how we feel, or what we really think, in a way that is comfortable for us is an extension of loving ourselves. It was a part of me that had been buried for such a long time. Finding my voice went hand in hand with discovering my power, but it can take a great deal of practice to get comfortable with speaking up.

On one occasion, I remember when a good friend of mine from high school asked me, "Why don't you answer me sometimes when I ask you a question? You're just silent." This took me by surprise; I had to really think about it. And honestly, in that moment, I didn't have a clue why I often resorted to silence. Looking back, I believe it was my way of coping with not feeling like my opinions mattered as much as hers.

I also found myself deferring to others to find out what their preference was first, and then responding with, "That's fine with me" and going along with whatever it was that they wanted me to do. Now I know that I am worthy of an opinion. Enlisting the help of my closest friends helped make me aware of how deferring to others had become my automatic response. It had gotten to the point where I was not considering my own choice or preferences at all. This way of thinking was not congruent with the message I was communicating to others and I was failing to honor myself.

While it has been a battle to find my voice, I have made great progress on being able to put into words how I am feeling. This transformation was furthered in great part by the help of my holistic doctor. However, the first step was acknowledging the problem when it happened. By taking note and realizing what is happening, you allow yourself an opportunity to correct it. Stating the phrase, "I need time to process how I am feeling and then I will get back to you," made a world of difference for me, and it can do the same for you.

This simple phrase gave me breathing space to get in touch with my feelings and find the exact words needed to express how I really felt. In the past, I would have simply buried my feelings and silenced my voice. Or, worse yet, I would have allowed others to tell me, "This is how it is going to be." I am constantly reminded of how physically good it feels to process my emotions, express myself, and then let it go. Gone are the days of storing all that toxicity within my body!

3. **Trust and Let Go** – As I saw how my life was unfolding, learning to trust and let go was imperative. The only healthy choice that I could think of was to move through the dark times that followed my NMO diagnosis. It was a painful time, and it provided a deep lesson for me to trust fully in a higher power.

Before then, I was accustomed to taking a backseat driver role in my own life. Even though I wanted to fully trust in God, I found myself trying to resist and retain some level of control from the back seat. Trusting is something I have had to work very hard at. That, along with "letting go and letting God"—especially after the possibility of losing my beloved career due to my health challenges—left me no other choice than to try and let go.

For me, this has been one of my greatest challenges in life. I like to think that if I just keep trying hard enough, I can steer things in the right direction, no matter what! I certainly found myself doing this in my marriage. I tried over and over again to make things work. But, if only one party is trying to create change, it just can't work.

The challenge of my misdiagnosis gave me the gift of finally taking my hands off the wheel. To learn that I had something else, something seen as far more serious, was shocking. My family's history of cancer disqualified me for all but one treatment, but even that door closed as I was ultimately unable to tolerate it due to life-threatening side effects. I was brought to my knees. It was finally in the embracing of this experience that I was able to move from fear into a peaceful place of trusting. I had no choice but to turn my difficulties over. When I was finally able to do so, it felt like a ton of bricks were lifted from my shoulders; I could breathe again!

A dear friend of mine, with the help of a talented artist, created a picture with the word T.R.U.S.T. spelled out with single stem roses. It is one of the most precious gifts I have ever been given. Receiving this gift lined up with my misdiagnosis; it was exactly what I needed precisely when I needed it. This beautiful piece now hangs directly across from my bed. It is the last thing I see before drifting off to sleep and it is the first thing I see when I wake in the morning.

4. **Discover Your Power** – Do things that make you feel good; that is the crux of discovering your power. I have a reminder on my phone that pops up once a day and asks, "What would make me feel good?" This has been a great way to remember to think about myself and indulge in self-love. This love may be as simple as spending a few minutes reading, sitting out by the ocean, or calling a friend.

Some days, this even means taking an extra little nap or going for a quiet walk if those are the things that will make me féel good. It reminds me to ask myself, "How does my body feel? What does it need from me today?" Checking your body's energy levels throughout the day reassures it that you have made it a priority.

This has been a huge change in my life as previously I was often frustrated and upset with my body due to overwhelming fatigue. No longer being able do the things I wanted would upset me, and in turn I began directing these resentments towards my body.

Something as simple as a common cold would frustrate me, because it had serious implications. I knew this meant that I would have to rest immediately or take on the risk of the dis-ease getting worse. But that all changed when I found my true power and the gift of putting myself first.

My first neurologist was extremely accomplished, and I am grateful for all of his insights. He was the one that first told me that my chances of having a flare-up significantly increased after contracting a simple virus like a common cold. I was fortunate to have him looking after me, as valuable information like this did not make it into many doctors' offices until several years later. I have been blessed over the years to have had the opportunity to work with incredible doctors, especially at times when I needed them most.

But that has not always been the case. I have also had troubling experiences with doctors that were less thorough than I needed them to be. It is of the utmost importance that you be your own best advocate and *search for the right doctor for you*. You must always feel confident about the care you are receiving, period!

It's All a Work in Progress

Some of the first questions you need to ask in order to start on the path to truly loving yourself are:

* What do I need for me?
* What makes me happy?
* What makes me unhappy?

70

When you start asking these questions, you will be amazed at the things you discover about yourself and your needs. Get curious and interested in what the path of truly loving yourself looks like for you.

Special Note: To assist with this task, I have a special gift that will help you on your way.

Simply visit http://www.freewellnessgift.com, and you will receive my "5 Keys To Discovering Your Personal Expression Of Self-Love."

I know that it will have an incredible impact. Enjoy!

Stay aware of your personal needs and make an effort to remind yourself to ask these questions on a routine basis. We need to make a conscious push to know ourselves and our needs fully before we can go to work on fulfilling them.

Discovering your power includes doing things for yourself and not just making sure that others' needs are met first. Back in my early days, I always put myself last in line. So while I was immersed in my own rebirthing process, I discovered the need to love myself like I would love a newborn baby. Take those immense feelings that blossom when holding a newborn, and turn that kind of deep, pure love and preciousness inward. Always keep in mind that we are simply a work in progress.

All of us deserve the kindness we give to others. I have discovered firsthand that nurturing the whole body, mind, and spirit will lead to a happier, healthier life, no matter what obstacles we may face. In fact, the biggest epiphany I have had along my journey is the necessity of truly loving myself, totally and unconditionally.

At some level, we are all aware of this. However, this important concept runs deep and there is a reason it is continuously mentioned throughout this book. The practice of loving ourselves is one that we cannot discuss too often, or hear too much about. You will come to realize by putting these words into practice that it is your heart that actually heals! We all have the Divine within us and as Dr. Wayne Dyer explained, this is the key to peace and power.

As I close out this chapter, let's take a moment to remember where it began and surrender to a higher power. I firmly believe that considering the Divine as love is a major key to our personal well-being. I even give my sadness to the Divine after I have had time to process those feelings. This way, I know that I have no need to hold on to them any longer. I have discovered that holding these negative emotions close, beyond the appropriate need to feel them, is toxic. The release and surrender allows us to live in the present. This is how you can keep your joy, your peace, and your happiness.

Shell 1: The Frequency of Abundance

66*Gratitude is the law of increase.*
*Complaint is the law of decrease.*99

– Florence Scovel Shinn

There is a common understanding that what we focus on is what we get more of. But, how do we do that? We hear all about getting on the frequency of abundance, but how do we get there? We make it happen by putting ideas into practice.

Is it true that we can get more of what we focus on?

Yes, absolutely this is true! Like attracts like and what you put your attention on is what you increase within your life. If you want more love in your life, focus on the things you love already. If you pay attention to all of the negativity on the news and TV, you will most assuredly attract more difficulties to complain about. This happens constantly, and our society is conditioned to believe it is acceptable to focus on what is wrong in the world; this negative outlook only perpetuates fear. I say we shift our focus and think mainly of the things that we love. This way of thinking provides a good deal more fun and joy for our lives!

So, how does this relate to abundance? Well, there is an abundance of *everything* in our world. Contrary to popular beliefs, there is more than enough to go around. That goes for both positive things and negative things.

The choice is yours - which would you prefer to have in your life?

Many times people are stuck in their old ways; even though they might want good things, their habits make it difficult for positivity to thrive. A negative internal environment makes it hard for positive thoughts to grow. Fortunately, life lessons can be found in every experience we have. Once a person has an awareness of what is really happening, they can make the conscious choice to decide if their life will be filled with positive and fulfilling substances or choose to forego those things. Contrary to popular belief, life does not "just happen" to us, but instead we create the situations and circumstances we find ourselves in.

How does that happen and are we in control?

There are plenty of books out there on this subject if you want to learn more. For now, it is important to know that you have way more control over your own life than you are likely giving yourself credit for. You choose your thoughts, no one else does that for you. Others may influence them, but the fact remains that you are the one in the driver's seat of your mind. Choose wisely and embrace empowering thoughts. It takes practice, but the reward is worth it.

The bottom line is that when you focus on gratitude and allow yourself to raise your vibrations in this way, you have no choice but to dwell in the frequency of abundance. This abundance is one that takes root in all things, including financial wealth, health and well-being, and amazing relationships with friends and family.

The more you focus on what is right in your life, the more that will go right for you. It might sound like magic, but it is backed by scientific studies! Try this practice for yourself, and see what unfolds within your own life. You will be happy with the results, that I can guarantee!

Shell 2: Raising Vibrations

> **"** *The only limits in our life are those we impose on ourselves.* **"**
>
> –Bob Proctor

Raising vibrations may sound like a daunting task, but it is all a matter of practice. In the evenings, right before we go to bed, is a great time to begin a nightly ritual. Practicing again in the early morning, just as you are beginning to wake, can lead to great success. The magical moment between wake and sleep is an incredibly powerful time.

What are some *specific* practices and daily rituals?

For me, I love to take time before drifting off to sleep to run through my day and give thanks for all the events that came my way. As I close each file in my mind, I express gratitude and love. By the time I arrive at the present moment, I am in a beautiful state of peace where I can softly transition to sleep. In the morning, just as I am beginning to wake, I give thanks for the amazing day that I am going to co-create with God. For me, this is a powerful way to begin each new day, one that is sure to be filled with a fresh new host of possibilities!

Be aware of how the words you use can be either powerful or not. Adding positivity to the words you choose can electrify them and make their impact immense. Make it a practice to select words with higher vibrations whenever you can and see your life change in the most miraculous ways. It is an easy practice to maintain, and the benefits stemming from it are vast.

Are there particular power words or affirmations that help?

Yes, there are many. But the question comes down to, "What words resonate with me?" Set aside a few minutes of quiet time, go within and test out certain words to see which ones have the greatest impact. Then, add those words to your daily practice and watch as they begin to have a profound effect on your day!

I also recommend practicing gratitude throughout the day. My go-to phrase is, "I am so deeply and profoundly grateful for…" and then I fill in the end of that sentence with all of the things that I am so grateful to have in my life. I even put in the things that I am seeking and turn this practice into an advance gratitude for the things that are coming my way. This helps bring those things to you faster and lays down a welcome mat for more good to come into your life.

Shell 3: Finding The Gift

66Dwell not upon what is lacking in your life, but regard those circumstances with gratitude. They pave the way for a shift in consciousness and conditions that put you in a position to manifest precisely what you have come into this lifetime to do.99

– Rasha

Putting faith in the fact that answers will unfold and that whatever I am going through is for a good reason is in itself a gift. I have also come to the understanding that additional gifts will reveal themselves in time. Knowing this brings an almost immediate sense of peace. It helps to calm me and reduce the stress that comes along with turbulent situations.

What about when bad things happen?
The onset of bad things is precisely when this kind of faith is critical. There is no other way to look at bad situations than to know that some good can come from it. This may be hard to embrace at first, especially when you are knee-deep and in the middle of it, but I believe there is always good that can

come from things initially seen as bad. The trick is to change our judgments and opinions of what defines the words "negative" and "bad." Keep an open mind and look for good to reveal itself.

Typically, for most challenging situations, there are several gifts you can look to receive. When something negative happens, remove yourself from the situation by looking at it from 10,000 feet up and creating some necessary space between you and whatever it might be. Make sure to always take the time to sit with it and look at it, even if you can't seem to find the gift at first.

Giving yourself this space is extremely helpful in allowing the gifts to reveal themselves. The space itself is a gift as it reveals a higher perspective. The key is to allow all of this to naturally unfold without having to paddle against the current. This process will most certainly support you in making the necessary decisions as you attempt to move through challenging situations.

What am I learning from this? How am I growing?

Again, we must always look for the gifts that are hidden within any challenging situations and circumstances. Ask yourself, repeatedly if necessary, "What can I learn from this, and how may I grow from this experience?" In the question lies the answers just waiting to be revealed. Stay positive and know that good can come from anywhere and from anything. Always try to expect the best and let go of the rest. Your body's health and well-being will thank and reward you for your positive attitude.

Oftentimes, the biggest gift in life is when something doesn't work out. Just know in the back of your mind that when you are allowing a situation to unfold, you are doing everything you need to do. You are not simply stepping back and letting everything fall apart, but are instead doing everything you feel needs to be done. There is some sense of peace in knowing and being aware that everything happens in a divine order. Then again, check in with yourself from time to time and ask, "What am I learning from this?" and "How am I growing?" Start to find the gift, and you will see just what a big difference it can make.

Shell 4: A Meaningful Practice

❝Gratitude is the magnificent and magical practice that infuses your entire being with a dose of richness.❞

– Kathryn Ford

I am always one to encourage my clients to find what works best for them. Even though I recommend and speak often of journaling, it is finding what resonates with you and moving forward with that which has the greatest impact.

Make sure that you are doing something, and make that something a part of your everyday practice. Again, it is guaranteed to make a significant impact upon your life, especially when it weaves an element of gratitude throughout. The magic of gratitude is great for both your overall health and well-being; I can promise you this.

How do we begin to heal?

Once again, start with gratitude. And remember, being grateful is as simple as it sounds! Shifting away from negative emotional patterns can directly benefit your health, says practicing cardiologist Mimi Guarneri M.D., medical director at the Scripps Center for Integrative Medicine. Anger, for instance, is extremely damaging to our well-being. However, it can be a challenge to channel difficult feelings, and she notes, "The hardest journey to make is the 18 inches from your head to your heart." In terms of healing one's self, this is where gratitude starts the process rolling, and is a suggested practice throughout each and every day.

We have now taken a look at several examples of practicing gratitude in our lives. Each of these examples focuses on what we have, and our inner pharmacy responds to this focus by releasing all kinds of sparkling, beautiful chemicals for our cells to bathe in. This goes a long way when it comes to gaining a sense of true wellness.

Grains of Sand:

As I look back and reflect on my life, I now realize that there was a better way to cope with negative emotions. Thankfully, I am now dealing with these emotions by facing them first. And then, once I have let them have their time, releasing them. In the past, I would store them in my body. And, as a result, they would only become stronger as I tried to push them back down.

I now understand that when I did this, my negative emotions were free to wreak havoc on my physical body. Instead of bottling up negative emotions, it is imperative that we work to find our voice and let them out. Otherwise, they can bring down our health and well-being.

For me, writing in a journal is a necessity and strongly complements being honest and letting the truth run free about what has been happening to me or how I feel. I had to learn to stop denying or sugarcoating my thoughts and feelings. Once these negative emotions were out in the open and exposed, there was opportunity to heal them.

Be Well! Exercise #3: In a journal, list at least three things you are grateful for each and every day. I recommend you do this first thing when you wake up each morning in order to set a beautiful tone for the rest of the day. Also, if it resonates with you, expand this practice into a journaling session and allow the beauty of expressing yourself on paper come to life. If you are currently engaging in one of these practices, I suggest you combine the two for a double dose of wellness!

Below is a list of suggestions to help you get started:

* Did you wake up and begin another day of life? Write down, "I am grateful for waking up and breathing another day into existence."
* Do you have children? Write down what you are grateful about for each of them, such as, "I am so very grateful to have Andrew in my life, as he brings so much joy to me each and every day."

* How is your health? Write down the parts of your health that you are grateful for, such as, "I am so grateful that my heart beats every minute and provides me with healthy blood circulation and such vitality."

Do this practice on a regular basis and turn it into a habit. When you do, you will see a significant shift in your overall health and well-being. If you want to take it a step further, increase your daily gratitude list to ten things you are grateful for. Have fun with this practice and enjoy the benefits to your health and well-being!

WAVE THREE
PEACE

Turning to the voice of wisdom within is where true inner peace resides. Peace is a choice and we need to make a conscious effort of choosing it often. It is what drives our emotional sense of well-being and supports our health. When you have peace, your body's natural pharmacy releases healthy chemicals, as opposed to the many toxic, stress-related ones that can bombard us each and every day if we allow them to.

It is inner peace that keeps us in balance. Finding ways to express ourselves openly and authentically—without outbursts or frustration—allows us to experience true inner peace. A calm resolve is vital to our health and well-being. We should guard our peace as we would a national treasure.

My Healing Journey

> ❝*Singing sad songs often has a way of healing. It gets the hurt out in the open and out of the darkness.*❞
>
> – Reba McEntire

After nearly 22 years with the same medical clinic, I had a persistent feeling that I needed to seek out a neurologist that specialized in multiple sclerosis. A strong pull led me to a neurology clinic with an MS center that specialized in cases like mine. It was a good thing that I followed my instincts, because they would reveal that I was really suffering from NMO, not MS as I had been told before. While having the truth out in the open provided an opportunity for change, it also carried its own overwhelming sea of emotions that brought me to my knees.

The Road Less Traveled

I already had a clinic in mind and was fortunate to have had a few second-opinion appointments with them over the years. But, since my insurance did not cover these visits, I saw them only when absolutely necessary.

Since I could no longer ignore my inner voice urging me to do so, I scheduled the first available appointment, which was about five months out. I knew this was what I needed to do, so I waited. Five months later, during my appointment, the specialist gave me a thorough physical exam, as well as taking an extensive health history of the past 22 years. He ordered several tests and asked me to return in a few weeks when the results were in.

Hiding Under the Bed

Resistance and Acceptance

❝*In life, go where it is warm and go towards the light.*❞
–Kathryn Ford

December 7, 2010, would prove to be a defining day in my life. It was one that would lead me down a road less traveled. It was a clear, cold, yet beautiful Minnesota day as I met with my new neurologist to discuss the test results and next steps.

The appointment began in typical fashion with a nurse intake followed by polite greetings from my new doctor. As he opened my chart on his computer, he stopped midsentence. His voice had some hesitancy to it, some uncertain surprise, as he said, "We have a problem here. You have tested positive for the NMO-IgG antibody and this changes everything. This test says that you in fact do not have multiple sclerosis, but rather neuromyelitis optica, otherwise known as NMO."

I looked at him with a mixture of worry and uncertainty. For most of my adult life, I thought I had MS. Now this doctor was going against my deeply-ingrained belief. "What!?" I said in confusion. It was clear by the look on his face that this was bad news. To confirm my suspicions, I asked, "I assume this is *not* something less severe than MS?" He looked down and away from me, and simply replied, "No. In fact, this disease can be much worse and much more devastating."

I felt numb. Due to the severity of NMO, he decided to repeat the blood test in case Mayo Clinic had mixed up my name and results. He asked me to go ahead and book a "family conference," as this was necessary protocol in order for him to proceed.

As Fate Would Have It

Just hearing the words "family conference" sent a shiver down my spine; there was a somberness to it. I wondered if my doctor needed to prepare my family for the devastating effects to come. I do not remember much after that, except I somehow managed to tell myself on the way home that there was still hope that something got mixed up; I prayed feverishly that Mayo Clinic made a mistake.

But they didn't. Their initial findings were confirmed and I felt like my life was over.

Fear about the future, which happens with all illness to some degree, is inevitable. As stated in the publication, *Inform MS,* dated 4/3/12, "MS continues and your life continues and they interact with and complicate each other." My ability to adjust to the challenges of this new dis-ease made a significant impact on the quality of my life despite other challenges I was facing.

Even after experiencing a great deal of loss in my life, I knew that things could be worse. Therefore, I chose to focus on my blessings, all of the things I was thankful for. As we explored in the last chapter, practicing gratitude has had a permanent positive impact on my life and I wouldn't give it up for the world. I focus on what makes me happy and what makes me feel good.

During another time of uncertainty in my life, I had the blessing of visiting one of my favorite places in the world - Marco Island, Florida. The ocean has always found ways to heal me, and this time was no exception. Even as I write these pages, I can feel the wonderful energy emanating from a crystal bowl full of shells on my desk.

When I arrived on the island, I had the privilege of meeting an artist who was giving painting classes. I had dabbled in painting as a child and, truth be told, I loved expressing myself in this way. Childhood memories flooded joy back into my spirit and I couldn't wait to get that brush back in my hand!

There are times where it feels like we cannot control any of the events happening in our lives. In these moments, it is necessary that we remember that we *get to control* how we respond to them. Creative expression, whether painting, journaling, or simply talking to a trusted friend, can formulate our ability to control how we respond. This ability to control our actions supports and allows us to move through the challenges. Then, we can seek out the light on the other side.

My emotions and feelings began to make their way onto the canvas. After thinking about what it was that I wanted to paint, I settled on some pink tulips. I love flowers and the color pink, and there was a simplicity to embracing the things I enjoy. It felt so good to think about something that brought me joy, something I could express through painting.

Pushing the Stormy Skies Away

It was a picture-perfect day and a tropical breeze was softly bringing freshness and rejuvenation to my heart. This would be my first experience painting outdoors, and I could feel that it was going to be God's perfect studio. My paintbrush began painting the scene, but my Higher Self gave it meaning.

After several days of therapeutic painting, with the healing sounds and sights of Marco Island supporting my inner being (along with a good deal of instruction and critiquing from my instructor!), the piece was finished. I received an amazing amount of positive feedback from both my fellow students and the instructor, but none of us really knew its true meaning and significance.

I was not able to discover its true meaning until I arrived home and had it framed and hung on the wall. One day, after some time had passed, I began to reflect on my work and fell deep into thought. It was at the end of meditating on the painting that the answer came to me—my painting was a metaphor for the most recent storms of my life!

The vibrant tulips in the foreground were huge and seemed to be pushing away the stormy skies above, crowding them right out of the picture. As it has been said many times before, the sun is always shining, you need only remove the clouds. My painting mirrored my own life, where I was in the midst of finding light through the darkness; it just required that I remove the clouds for the storm to subside. What a blessing!

I had stopped resisting and began accepting what was happening in my life, making a conscious decision to make the best of it. It was not the life that I had planned for myself, but it was the life that was waiting for me. I would move forward, always looking ahead to a bright future. Years later, I would understand this to be my purpose in life. I would make it my life's work to help others find the same peace in the midst of their own storms.

In Control of My Reactions

As I reflect on those days spent painting on Marco Island, I have to marvel about how everything unfolded so naturally. Gratitude for all the events in my life is my daily expression, and I would not be the person I am today without the trials. Much pain and loss have marked the pages of my life, but the many gifts of love, especially the love and compassion I have for myself, shine so much brighter. Remember to love yourself through all the challenges and storms you face. Love *always* shines brighter.

I had to learn to be gentle with myself, and I encourage you to do the same. By practicing gentleness, you will find a greater awareness of what is happening and what the most appropriate response might be. Always remember to take a moment to be still and to just breathe.

It is in this stillness that we are able to lean into gratitude. In modern psychology, there is research from the University of Pennsylvania that shows expressions of gratitude improves our immune systems. A practice of gratitude includes looking for the good in the moment, looking for good in the person you are with, and looking for the good that resides in present activities. However, these are just some examples of striving for excellence. The stars are the limit for the many ways you can practice gratitude!

One of the several post-it notes I have put on my bathroom mirror reads, "Keeping my energy field as high as possible is top priority!" Creating reminders to quickly refocus and regroup after obstacles have undercut our all-important energy fields can give us the jolt we need to bring them back to full capacity.

The first thing I do upon waking is to say, "Thank you God for the amazing day I am going to co-create with you." This sets the tone for peace throughout the day and reminds me of the important principles I strive to live by. First, **all** is truly good, and the events of our lives are **all** good for our soul's evolution. Second, it reminds me that I am in complete control of how I respond to each event in my life. I get to choose how I interpret it. I can choose how I feel about the things happening in my life. I have the power to make this day amazing! I have the power to choose peace.

We pay a large price for allowing ourselves to reside in negative energy fields. When we understand that our entire life is based upon our energy field, we can wrap our arms around the importance of keeping it as high as possible. The more aware you are of your energy field, the easier it is to make it a priority. Checking in with it almost becomes second nature after just a little practice. I encourage you to use the post-it idea for your bathroom as a gentle reminder. It really works!

Letting Go of the Security Blanket

"Some people believe holding on and hanging in there are signs of great strength. However, there are times when it takes much more strength to know when to let go and then do it."

– Ann Landers

My parents and I traveled to Mayo Clinic to meet with one of the world's foremost experts on NMO. Our goal was to discuss treatment options and to see what perspective a second opinion might hold. My mother, a nurse practitioner, has always been a significant help when dealing with the medical community. She knows the right questions to ask and understands the medical terms that might otherwise pass right over my head. She has truly been my angel.

The start of this experience closely mirrored my other office visit; I had my intake with a nurse, followed by a meeting with a doctor who conducted a complete exam, and then I was finally face to face with the expert I was so eager to meet. You might remember before that there was a Mayo Clinic doctor who was stunned to see how well I was doing. Well, this is the very same one! He said, "You don't even look like someone who has had MS for 22 years, let alone NMO." He then encouraged me to share what I was doing for my condition with others. He was the first of several doctors to urge me to share my health triumphs and the practices that had been making such a difference.

But, despite his positivity, what he said next was hard to hear. He was straight to the point about the severity and seriousness of NMO. Several times, the fear inside me was so tight that it was hard to breath. He let me know that while I appeared to be doing well for someone with my condition, things could change at any moment.

Our Minds Are Very Powerful

It was at this point that he let me know the injections I had been taking for MS—ones that were full of painful side effects—were actually harmful for someone with NMO. I closed my eyes and allowed the flood of emotions to surge through me. I remember thinking, "What? How can this be happening? Dear God, when am I going to wake up from this horrible nightmare?" I had feelings of anger rush through me for all of the damage my previous treatments had done.

But that was not the life I wanted to live.

I opened my eyes, took a breath, and let him know that my mind was very powerful. I had believed that those injections had done me a great deal of good, and I believed that my body had responded to that positively; I know they didn't hurt me. He smiled at me and said, "We're sticking with that!"

The first thing we needed to do was change my medication. The new treatment would be an infusion that I would receive at Mayo Clinic. It would be two infusions, two weeks apart, twice a year. This new medication also came with a lengthy list of possible side effects, some of which could be terminal.

Even so, in order to make sure I was a candidate for the infusions, initial tests were necessary. Once the green light was given, these infusions would be administered and continue indefinitely. Despite the uncertainty of the future, I found myself holding dear to a strange sense of relief; we had a plan.

As my father drove us home, I relaxed into a state of peace. My mother and I discussed the most important parts of the appointment, including how I needed to stop my injections immediately.

For so long I had held on to the belief that these injections were my saving grace, and it was frightening to give them up even though we were told that they were harmful for me. On the other hand, about a year earlier, I had a gut feeling that I was not supposed to be on the injections, but I never acted on those feelings.

My gut was telling me to listen to the Mayo expert and stop the injections immediately. But again, I admit there was a strange sense of security with the injections that had become such a big part of my life. In actuality, I was scared of letting them go. They were all I had to cling to for so many years. Sometimes the negative things in life are hard to let go of, especially when they are all you know. But it was the right thing to do.

After the preliminary test results came back, I was given the green light to go forward with the infusions. Plans were made for May 10, 2011. The alarm went off early that day and we started the hour-and-a-half trip to Mayo Clinic. I was so grateful that a friend accompanied me for the visit, as my fears of being able to tolerate the new medication were racing through my mind. What was going to happen to me?

Before I knew it, I was going over highlights of the treatment and what to expect one final time before receiving it. The meeting went smoothly, but it was so much information at once. I began questioning myself and felt anxious about whether I really understood everything. Having my close friend there helped; her presence was the reassurance I needed.

A few years ago, my friend with breast cancer faced a similar challenge following a doctor's appointment and called me to express her frustration. She indicated that even though her husband and sister accompanied her to the appointment, they could not agree on many of the doctor's points while driving home. It was as if each individual heard something different. Based on our past experiences and how difficult situations affect us, that isn't so far from the truth! I told her that this was actually a blessing in disguise, because it gave her an opportunity to call the doctor and get clarification, rather than making assumptions.

Our next hurdle was to find the Infusion Center. My friend, thankfully, took over and found the way. What happened next was a personal reassurance to me. I have always found that my spiritual number is "3." Not only was I the third "Kathryn" called by the nurse in the waiting room, but the infusion took place in room 21, which in numerology adds up to 3 (2+1=3). It may not seem like much, but it offered me some peace as I was given pre-infusion medication to help with some of the side effects. Finally, after many unsuccessful attempts, the I.V. was administered and we were ready to get underway.

My friend and I said a prayer and again a sense of relief flooded over me as I watched the clear liquid enter my body. I visualized this medication as a great cleansing for my body, and I grounded myself firmly within a state of gratitude for the purification.

The Best Laid Plans

Due to the serious nature of the treatment, a nurse closely monitored me and ensured that the infusion was given very slowly. But even under her watchful gaze, complications began to appear a few hours after we started. I finally had to ask for something to relieve at least some of the excruciating pain. However, much to my surprise, I was told no, as my doctor did not want to mask how my body was responding. My reactions were giving them valuable information.

To combat the extreme pain, the speed at which the medication was being administered was slowed down, which helped my heart recover from feeling as if it was about to jump from my chest. While the pain and other strange feelings were still present in my back, I was told that the procedure was going well.

This was my first time receiving this concentrated medicine, and my doctor was pleased with my tolerance. My friend had slipped out of the room to get lunch, and while she was gone I planned to try to get some rest. Unfortunately, the pain kept on, so the best I could do was close my eyes and focus on all of the good that this new medication was doing for me.

The Best Medication on the Planet

Shortly thereafter, I opened my eyes to see my friend entering the room with a huge bouquet of flowers. While a beaming smile stretched across my face, I told the nurse that I had just received one of the best prescriptions ever. Other nurses entered the room and admired what I felt was the best medication on earth - the feelings of love and support! With a handful of extra challenges before the day was done, I had made it through the day and we made our way home. I did it! I survived!

As mentioned several times before, the autoimmune dis-ease diagnosis in many ways was a gift to me, one that I am so glad I finally opened. For years, I left it hiding under my bed. And yet, after a period of time spent in denial, I slowly opened the card, read it, and saw the beauty in the wrapping. I began to understand how my already deep spiritual connection could become even deeper. I saw how much it pushed me to treasure each day and how I naturally began to live more in the present moment. I stopped putting things off and slowly began enjoying more of the little things in life. And, wouldn't you know that those are the things I have found to be the most important things in life.

A quiet moment in meditation appreciating the pure silence, a deep gaze at a single beautiful flower, the tender touch of someone special, or a serene walk in nature experiencing God's miraculous creation. These moments are healing to every cell in our bodies and provide us with the perfect prescription for well-being, even in times of trouble.

Crisis Management

Don't Let Your Fears Paralyze You

❝Be faithful to that which exists within yourself.**❞**

– Andre Gide

We would repeat the treatment two weeks later. This time, I experienced fewer side effects to go along with the medication. At least that's how it seemed at first.

Over the following months, I would face challenges that would prove to be defining for me and my journey. I felt as if a truck had run over me. I was not digesting my food and constantly felt ill.

NMO is a problem with your B cells and the drug infusion literally wiped out all of mine. Theoretically, that is a good sign when it comes to NMO, but it damaged much of my tissue in the process. As a result, harmful agents usually corralled by our B cells were left to run rampant.

Within a few months, a number of scary surprises seemed to jump out at every turn. From a mole that needed to be removed because of questionable cells to cysts that were forming in my body, a couple of which were found in breast tissue, these were troubling times. While waiting on test results to confirm whether or not one of the cysts in my breast tissue was indeed cancerous, I knew that I needed to keep practicing the prescriptions of gratitude and self-love that held me so heavily up to this point.

After only two infusions, I had already experienced several brushes with abnormal or precancerous cells, which struck me as something to be addressed. I called my then neurologist to report what was happening. I told him that I felt it was a result of the new infusion medication.

Ironically, years earlier, I decided to undergo a prophylactic bilateral mastectomy due to my strong family history of breast cancer. Experts agreed that I had a higher chance of getting breast cancer given those hereditary factors, and there was concern that I may not be able to tolerate the drugs used to fight breast cancer, mainly due to the fact that I was thought to have MS.

Because of this, the doctor performing the aspiration said that he had never seen a cyst develop like this in someone who had already undergone a mastectomy. I started to feel like I was living in a doctor's office. I was in a constant state of either having tests done or waiting for results.

At any given time, we all have troublesome cells in our bodies. Fortunately, for the most part, we have the defenses necessary to take care of them. It was my belief that the infusions were leaving me defenseless and these brushes with cancer were a result of that. After expressing my concerns, I was taken back when my doctor told me these health outbursts were not related and I should keep to the infusion schedule. I could *not* believe my ears!

What Happened Next Shocked Me Even More

At one point, my doctor even told me that if I went off the medication, I would be "making the biggest mistake of my life." I would face the risk of becoming blind and confined to a wheelchair in the near future.

I responded with, "Doctor, with all due respect, if I am dead we do not need to worry about the NMO!" He was surprised at how I stood up for myself and had expressed my feelings in the way I did. But he said in an extremely firm voice, "Don't let your fears paralyze you!"

I thought to myself, "I feel like you are trying to paralyze me with fear right now!" The conversation was going nowhere. The doctor was becoming more and more upset with me and unfortunately there were no other drugs available.

I felt the best thing to do was to tell him that I needed time to think about it and I would get back to him. Even though our conversation was deeply upsetting, I knew in my heart that he was being firm because he really did care about me and only wanted the best for me. I knew his harsh, strong approach was simply his belief that I would be making a catastrophic mistake if I stopped the infusions. All in all, I am certain his intentions were good.

I was no stranger to experiencing loss or facing challenges. When I was in my late 30's, I felt a different kind of pain. This type of pain is felt when a significant piece of one's identity is taken from them. I found myself at the point where my physical condition made it so I was no longer physically able to continue working. I was devastated as I had been extremely creative in holding on to the career in human resources that I loved so much. I had worked so hard to get to where I was, and I readily admit that it had become a huge part of my personal identity.

I received a tremendous amount of personal satisfaction from my work, and I had grown to love the level of responsibility and complex problem-solving that were just two of the benefits the job delivered to me on a regular basis. When someone asked me what I did for work, I would tell them that most of the time I was a firefighter, putting out one fire after another, and loving every minute of it!

Over time, I had transitioned from working 60+ hours a week to a job-share arrangement and, finally, to a part-time position. Being resourceful, I had decided to take the bus to work in Minneapolis in order to conserve my energy for the workday. This arrangement also let me rest while returning home in the evening! One particularly exhausting day, I asked the bus driver to wake me at my stop as I did not want to open my eyes and realize I was in Timbuktu!

These kind of moments were embarrassing for me and it was difficult to face losing much of my independence. But, in the name of creative problem-solving and in the face of true desperation, I pushed through. I would do whatever I could to keep something that meant so much to me - a career that I loved.

As the fatigue grew more severe, I had no choice. I couldn't continue. My condition had escalated to debilitating, and I was overwhelmed and had sustained an extreme exhaustion that decreased my capacity for functioning.

The fear of losing my career and facing a life filled with more and more isolation was frightening. When I finally had no other option but to stop working, my first thought was, "My life has come to an end." If you or a loved one has felt something similar, please take some comfort in knowing that you are not alone. What I can tell you, and I am living proof of, is that there is a way to get better!

After I had allowed pain to have its time, I realized that my life had not ended; I simply would not allow it to end! I know what it is like to suffer and to feel hopeless and helpless, but I also know how it feels to be empowered enough to regain my sense of well-being. Mostly, it takes willpower and determination.

Standing with My Back Against the Wall

❝Faith is seeing light with your heart when all your eyes see is darkness.❞

– Decaleco

So, although you can see that in my late 30's I thought I had been through the worst, I was reminded again that everything is relative. I now see that the gift in all of these difficult situations has been a lesson about priorities and a reminder to me that it was time to put the focus on my health and well-being.

With that said, I can see that the events of my life have all been carefully orchestrated in order to lead me down my soul's highest path. Now, let's jump back to being faced with the decision of whether or not to continue the infusions that I felt were quite possibly going to kill me. One of the major gifts I received from this experience was to live out the opportunity of choosing to listen to my higher self, even when I could not find a single doctor who would support my beliefs. I was up against a wall and initially felt very much alone. But then I realized I had the greatest doctor in the universe on my side. It was up to me to do one thing, listen.

The following is my best recollection of how this life-changing series of events unfolded. At the same time, I was prescribed the infusions by my doctor, I attended a conference in Los Angeles for NMO patients. It was at this conference that I had the opportunity to speak with a doctor from Johns Hopkins who was widely considered an expert on NMO. During a break, I introduced myself, explained my dilemma, and asked what he would advise his wife to do if she were in my shoes.

He thought for a minute and then said, "Kathryn, the way I see it, you are going to have to stay on the medication to treat your NMO and then fight the cancers as they come up." Again, I just about fell over; it took everything I had in me to keep my composure. I returned to my seat and didn't really "hear" anything else that was happening for the next couple of hours or so.

My life felt like a painful cycle. I was constantly finding new problems, having the necessary tests and procedures, and then—worst of all—waiting for the results. After the cysts in my breast, which were an almost impossible problem after the mastectomy I had undergone, I had pretty much had enough.

Sometimes it takes a lot of information for an answer to come through. Clearly and loudly, it hit me. I had been praying for a sign, a really big sign, ever since my medication dilemma had started. I had wanted a sign so big so that I could not miss it. Well, this was my sign! I knew in my heart that I could not live this way any longer. I had to find a path to not only survive, but to thrive.

Finding Peace Within the Fear

My life had become a battlefield of fear and negativity. I was backed against a wall and the only thing I could think to do was to surrender to God, fully and completely. I simply did not know where to turn, so I went within and started on my true journey.

Honestly, I think this was the first time in my life that I had given up the need to direct any part of the process. I asked Him for clear guidance to know what to do. I was humbled and brought to my knees. When I listened to my feelings, my heart, and my intuition, thoughts of focusing on health and promoting a healthy lifestyle were where I found peace and calm.

I found a sense of "this is the correct choice for you, Kathryn," and I knew I had to find the courage to go down the path less traveled. Robert Frost's words, pulled from *The Road Not Taken*, spoke my truth:

"Two roads diverged in the woods, and I took the one less traveled by… and that made all the difference."

Here I was, going against some of the world's most highly-regarded authorities on health, and I knew I was doing the right thing. I looked to other doctors for support, but each deferred to Mayo Clinic and agreed with the earlier findings and recommendations.

In one particularly heated consultation, which brought me to tears, I shared with another neurologist that I had decided to take a holistic approach and to focus on health instead of dis-ease. I told him that it was my hope that he would still be there for me should I have a full blown exacerbation and need immediate intervention with a procedure called plasmapheresis.

After vehemently disagreeing with my decision to discontinue conventional treatment, he finally agreed to stay on as my neurologist. At the end of the appointment, as we both walked out of the office, he apologized for making me cry. He stated again that he disagreed with my decision, but if I found something that worked, to please let him know so that he could pass the information on to other patients.

As I walked to my car, the realization of what had just happened dawned on me. The appointment and discussions were primarily about protecting him from legal recourse; he now had the documentation in my chart that showed he was doing everything he could to look after me. It was only at the end of the visit that he showed his compassion, laying out the enormous concern he had for all of his patients; he wanted each and every one of them to find healing. When reading between the lines, I could see that there was nothing else he could offer me at the time. He was genuinely interested in any information I would come across, especially because it could have the potential to help his other patients as well.

I believe this conversation gave me an opportunity to be stronger than I had ever been before. I became closer to the Infinite and found an even deeper sense of trust. And I knew with every cell of my being that I was being guided by the Divine.

At the End, there is Also a Beginning

Part of that inspiration blossomed in an effort to reach out to leaders already making a difference in the lives of those with NMO. Below is a portion of the letter I sent to Victoria Jackson of the Guthy-Jackson Charitable Foundation, an organization that focuses on NMO. Victoria had started her foundation when her then fifteen-year-old daughter had been diagnosed.

Dear Victoria,

I am writing to express my extreme gratitude for the gift of you and the Guthy Jackson Foundation.

… It has been a dream of mine to write a book for people with health challenges, and to give them the tools to thrive and live a life of excellence. I guess the book now has an additional chapter - the misdiagnosis. I have a wealth of information I have gathered over the years, both conventional and alternative, and I know that by practicing these, and living a lifestyle that promotes health, my outcome has been directly affected in a positive way.

I believe it is my purpose in life to serve others and one way I can help is through this book. If I can help someone else through what I have learned on my journey, then all is well indeed! You and your daughter have done that for me and the help I received from you has made a huge impact on this new "chapter" in my life's journey.

Even though I was learning and growing as a person, it should be pretty obvious that I often had an overwhelming amount of fear associated with my NMO diagnosis. The fear was so severe that I was not always sure if I was going to be able to move forward. At times, it was nothing short of paralyzing.

In her book, *Yes! Energy*, author and coach Loral Langemeier states that, "Stress is when you lose faith and replace it with fear." I clearly see that this is precisely what I did following the NMO diagnosis. And yet, the fear began to subside with the loving support of precious family and friends and with the discovery of organizations such as the Guthy-Jackson Charitable Foundation. For this I am eternally grateful.

Treatment choices and complements to treatments

I encourage you to choose your course of treatments wisely. By this I mean that all conventional and complementary practices must resonate with you. Whatever it is, do it out of love for yourself. Listen to your inner voice and make sure you are not going forward out of fear. It must feel right to you and in harmony with your inner being.

The best way I have found to decipher which treatments are in alignment with me is to get in touch with how I feel inside when I think about a specific treatment. I will also do muscle testing, more formally known as applied kinesiology, as I have found this to be highly accurate. Many chiropractors, naturopaths, medical doctors, nurses, physical therapists, or other healthcare workers are trained in this specialty and can use it to complement your other treatment regimes. In the end, we must always remember that if it doesn't feel right, there is always another way.

At some point, we have all heard that "Information is power." I believe it is not only powerful, but for me personally, it has also been a means to calm my nerves. I am the type of person who feels much better knowing what I am dealing with. That knowledge allows me to begin finding solutions that support and allow my entire being to move forward in a positive manner.

I also know that happiness is an inside game, and that no matter what is happening around us, it is possible to take our power back. I knew I could transform my prognosis and I did just that.

These transition zones in our lives are truly sacred and where we grow the most. For me, it was a gradual process of forming a new and different life. As I have done after each new health crisis, I moved forward and became whole again along the way.

Before closing out this chapter, I would like to touch on another tool for finding peace. I was introduced to this practice though the following question: "What do I know that I am pretending not to know or am denying that I do know?"

Several years ago, on a beautiful day in March, a dear friend— whose timing seems to flirt with perfection—first sent me this question. It was on that particular day that I needed to ask myself what answers I was hiding from in order to move forward with my life. What perfect timing!

Allowing the Answers to Arrive

She said that we are supposed to ask the question, then let it go. The answer would arrive in its own time. The perfect timing of the universe is amazing, and its constant love is always there to help those who ask. Case in point, I had just finished meditating on an extremely challenging issue when that message arrived.

As I concentrated on "I am that I am" and "I am power" during my meditation, I also asked God to help me to know how to move forward in this particular situation. I was feeling as though I was failing to make a positive impact on the seemingly endless conflict.

When I received the above message, I could not believe the timing. This was exactly what I needed to ask and, even though it might be difficult, be honest with myself about it. After some reflection, I realized that one thought in particular came up several times: "I am doing something that I have done in previous relationships. I am trying to impose my best wishes for the person onto them." Wow, really powerful insight for sure.

I needed to honestly acknowledge this, because it was one of the main reasons for my frustration. I decided to follow my friend's advice by asking the question and then letting the answer arrive in its own time. It arrived exactly when it was supposed to and I let my gratitude run free.

Shell 1: My Natural Pharmacy

"Peace is a journey of a thousand miles and it must be taken one step at a time."

–Lyndon B. Johnson

Peace drives our emotional sense of well-being and directly affects our health. When we experience peace, our bodies' natural pharmacies release all kinds of healthy, beautiful chemicals to drown out toxic stress-related chemicals. That feeling of peaceful freedom creates an environment for health and well-being to thrive! Peace is a choice, and we need to make a conscious effort to choose it often.

Is being happy a key element to achieving a peaceful body?
Yes, it is. The bottom line is that we are all looking for the things that make us happy and for even more happiness to be present within our lives. Naturally, when we are happy and our positive emotions are flourishing, our health and well-being improve and it goes a long way to maintaining our youthfulness. Simply put, being happy helps your body find more peace throughout the day.

My goal is to put myself and my health first by not allowing anything to upset my peace. Again, I have not achieved perfection, however, I am always improving at remembering my goal in the midst of negativity.

Can I really make a difference in how I feel physically?

Absolutely! If nothing else, this should be your main takeaway from this book. You have more power over your condition than you give yourself credit for. Your attitude and positive outlook can make a huge difference in how your physical body feels. Do not take this lightly, as this is a big key to your success in health and overall well-being. Stay open to possibility and allow the greater good to come through and pour into your entire physical being. It will make a difference, and the results will make themselves clear over time.

When my life feels like it has fallen into chaos, I like to retreat into the "eye of the storm." This is the peaceful place we all have within and is accessible at any time. After all, our thoughts today will create our futures.

Now, how about that for some motivation! You have the power to be your own best advocate and to prescribe what is best served in terms of your health and well-being. So, remember to stay positive and do what brings you happiness and joy in your life. The more fun and laughter, the better!

Shell 2: Guarding My Peace

"If anything interferes with my inner peace, I will walk away. Arguments with family members. All that stuff. None of it matters."

– Shirley MacLaine

For me, finding peace is priceless; guarding my peace like it's Fort Knox has helped me realize just how important it is. It is a treasure that has done wonders for my overall health and well-being. That is why I make conscious choices to allow peace in my life each and every day.

What does it mean to stand guard over my mind?

There is a power in being watchful over what thoughts, feelings, and emotions you allow to occupy your mind. You are like an English guard that protects the Queen of England, always alert and making sure that nothing harmful enters the palace. Your mind is a treasure that needs to be protected and cared for 24/7. Treat it as such and only allow peaceful and loving activity through the gates.

When we choose peace and turn it into a full-fledged practice, we are able to ward off the storms life throws our way. I find that an emphasis on peace lessens so much of the pain that comes with the difficult times in life. When choosing peace, we respond from a calm and collected state of being rather than reacting from and being in a state of fear. Then, I am able to be more levelheaded in my thinking and remind myself that my inner peace directly affects my overall health and well-being.

Since there is no way for any of us to control the weather patterns of this world, from time to time we will encounter stormy weather. It is how we prepare for those storms and how we react to them that matters most. Stand guard and keep your inner peace at the forefront at all times; you will quickly see how this approach promotes great benefits to your overall health.

How do you come at it from being "in the eye" of the storm?

I make a conscious choice to face what I am experiencing. I release any controlling thoughts over the outcome, and focus on what I would love to have happen. I embrace all of the good that will be revealed through the experience and know that I am, on some level, a strong and willing participant in the situation. By welcoming the good and knowing that I am protected in all things, I can stay in the center of the storm. And here, in the eye, there is no chaos. It is calm and I choose to allow good things to flow through me at all times.

So how do you do that? What does it look like? Know that this approach doesn't mean that I never get upset. But, many years ago, I would hold the upset in and equate that with finding—or keeping—

my inner peace. I would think that if I didn't react or let it out, if I didn't let the anger or hurt come barging out, then I was remaining peaceful. But that was not true! That way of thinking only allows the troubles to fester.

Shell 3: The Wellness Priority

> **"**Learn to float over the turbulent sea and not become dragged down into the depths of it, where you fear you may perish. You will not perish. You will simply be made to suffer—unnecessarily.**"**

– Rasha

While my outer shell seemed peaceful, my insides were writhing in uncertainty. Once I became aware of my incorrect definition of peace, I was able to find a beautiful ability to use my words to diffuse the things that make me upset when the time is appropriate. And, I have learned just how healthy it can be to let these worries and frustrations out.

I can be upset on the outside, and still know that my inner peace is protected. Release what needs to be released. For me, the healthy way of doing this is not yelling or screaming, but expressing my concerns in a calm and patient manner. It is worth repeating just how important it is to be who we are and to say how we feel.

Is there a way to express myself without being upset or angry?

Yes, of course there is. The trick is to take a moment to collect your thoughts *before* you blurt something out that is fueled by highly-charged emotions. Most often we regret what is said in the heat of battle. If we are to instead take a precious breath and give ourselves the gift of time to gather our thoughts, we will create more peace and harmony in our relationships with others.

This does not mean that we should allow others to walk over or abuse us in anyway. It simply means that there is so much goodness in taking a moment to consciously choose our responses rather than reacting out of hurt, fear, or anger. Once we slow our reaction time and give ourselves a buffer zone to respond, we can see the overall situation a bit more clearly and find a more loving response to whatever initiated the anger or upset.

Even if something is upsetting, it does not have to upset you to the core. Remember, what we suppress eventually gets expressed, and this expression can dictate the effect an event has on our health. It is our bodies' way of finally being heard.

The goal here is to find healthy solutions to the everyday stressors that we encounter. This provides us an alternative to handcuffing our own bodies and preventing them from doing what they do best - keeping us healthy and whole.

It is much better to be proactive and find healthy practices that support your body and its natural way of being. The alternative, as mentioned, is neither fun nor pretty, and—as evidenced in my own case—can be rather painful and restrictive. Making your wellness a priority is a must!

As I have often heard it said, listen to your body when it is still whispering to you to make a change. Don't wait until it picks up a hammer to hit you over the head as a wake-up call instead!

How can I better control my reactions to outside disturbances?

For many, the trick is to ask yourself telling questions before you react to a situation. For example, I have often heard the phrase, "What would love do?" If you take a moment to see the disturbance for what it is, and many times it stems from a cry for help in one way or another, you will allow yourself the gift of time to see all of the responses you can choose from.

Again, a buffer zone is helpful to make it more clear what is really going on. If you were to only react with love, what would you do? If you were to step into the shoes of another, what would you see? With more love and compassion, it is amazing just how easy it is to face these so-called disturbances and react in a healthy way.

In situations when I feel like I am not being respected, or where I am perhaps feeling wronged, it is so freeing to say what is on my mind in a way that is comfortable to me and true to my authentic self. It is important to our health to express how we feel and, of course, to respect the other person at the same time. The liberation of having control over your responses is exhilarating.

Shell 4: Freedom to Choose

66 Choose your thought carefully. Keep what brings you peace, release what brings you suffering. And know that happiness is just a thought away.99

– Nishan Panwar

I believe that we have the freedom to choose how we respond as long as we decide our reactions consciously. We are either allowing the kind of life that happens to us, or we are living a life where we create our own future. What we need is to be elevated out of a victimhood mentality, one that tells us, "I have no control over this," and into knowing that we have 100% control over our thoughts, how we respond, and the choices we make.

What if freedom of choice conflicts with deep-rooted beliefs?

This is a tough discussion. I would suggest to once again keep an open mind. There is a great mentality that states, "If you think you know everything there is to know of how this world works, well then, you simply know nothing at all." Solid beliefs may be at the root of your personal foundation, but they are only helpful if they are not so rigid that they cannot be re-evaluated to determine if they are serving your needs in a healthy and life-giving way. Remain open to new ideas and new ways of being, and keep evaluating as you go.

The point is that we have way more control over our lives than meets the eye. Added to that is the reality that we do not have to hold pain and suffering inside our bodies. It is my belief that we have the ability to liberate ourselves into greater health and well-being, just by being mindful of our thoughts, feelings, and actions. We have the capacity for true inner peace.

How do I keep myself from falling back into old patterns?

Practice, practice, and more practice. Teach yourself to send unconditional love inwards until it becomes your very nature. Keep your eyes open and take note of habits and patterns. Be aware and open to changing what no longer serves you in your new healthy and peaceful lifestyle. Choose empowering ways of being and never beat yourself up when you slip back into old habits. This is a practice, one that over time will become your new normal way of living, so be kind to yourself.

I recommend you be kind and gentle with yourself, no matter what! This is the basis of everything I teach. As is the case with anything new, there is a learning curve. You will not be perfect right out of the gate and there are times that old patterns will, and do, show up. Stay in practice and keep choosing new and more empowering thoughts. And then, just watch the magic begin to show up in your life and have incredible effects on your health!

Grains of Sand:

First and foremost, we must remain positive and come out from hiding under the covers when things are not going as well as we would like. Even when difficult news is presented, stay calm and look for the good in the situation; don't forget that it can often be hidden in plain sight. Learn to accept the things you cannot control and let your fears go. When we pause to gather our thoughts before reacting, we are in a better position to handle stressful situations with ease and grace.

And at all times, remember that the power of your mind and the thoughts you think on a regular basis can and do have a profound effect on your health and well-being. Even so, the best laid plans can go astray and detours are sometimes necessary, so give yourself a big dose of love and understanding when they crop up. Then, start back on your journey towards a better and more grand existence. To recap:

* Release what no longer serves you
* Never let your fears paralyze you
* Ask questions and allow the answers to arrive in their own time
* Guard your inner peace as something precious

Once you become comfortable with these new practices and behaviors, you will be witness to the miracle of your own rebirth. With dedication and concentration, your thoughts, feelings, and emotions will become your health's barometers, if not your greatest allies. Again, have fun with these practices and enjoy the life they bring!

WAVE FOUR
SELF-WORTH

When the dark night of the soul—the moment where we find life's greatest gifts in the midst of trials—appears in our lives, we are given an opportunity to strengthen our sense of value and self-worth. Will we crumble under the pressures and criticisms of the past? Or will we rise from the ashes of doubt and blame to emerge as a better version of ourselves? So much of the outcome depends on the level of forgiveness we allow ourselves to give and receive.

Self-worth is one of the most important aspects of our health and well-being. With a positive opinion of ourselves, we can move mountains. However, if we see ourselves in a negative light, we may be resolved to remain stagnate, leaving little room for movement. It is always our choice as to what we think and believe to be true. So let's choose wisely!

Dark Night of the Soul

In This Chapter

* Finding the light when all you see is darkness
* Accepting responsibility while you regain love and confidence

66*When we change the way we look at things, the things we look at change.*99

- Wayne Dyer

This wave's theme is self-worth, which just so happens to be one of the most important aspects of our health and well-being. If we are equipped with a positive opinion of ourselves and our potential, we can move mountains. However, if we allow a negative opinion to take charge, we may push our thoughts and aspirations into a lonely and dark cave, one where we limit our experiences and growth.

We are not born with a positive sense of self-worth, as it is a learned behavior and attribute. However, we always have the choice of what we think and believe to be true when it comes to who we are.

Over the years, we may have friends, well-meaning family members, teachers, and others tell us who we are and what our worth is to them. But that is not what matters most at the end of the day. More important than their opinions are what we believe to be true about ourselves and whether or not we hold on to a positive sense of self-worth.

Again, the key is to be our own best advocate and build our own self-worth to levels that allow us to thrive. This leads us to a healthy life, both on the inside and outside.

The Power of Relationships

When we choose to have a significant other in our lives, that relationship has the potential to make a major and direct impact on our health. It is up to each specific relationship whether that impact is positive or negative. It is imperative for our overall health and well-being that our most intimate relationships are genuinely healthy and contribute in a way that supports our spirit. If a significant relationship is not healthy, it will weigh you down and contribute to a lessened sense of self-worth.

On top of that, these negative—or possibly even toxic—relationships will deplete one's self-worth all the way down to the cellular level. Candace Pert, Ph.D., states in her book, *Molecules of Emotion*, "I've come to believe that virtually all illness, if not psychosomatic in foundation, has a definite psychosomatic component."

She continues with, "Recent technological innovations have allowed us to examine the molecular basis of the emotions and begin to understand how the molecules of our emotions share intimate connections with, and are indeed inseparable from, our physiology. It is the emotions, I have come to see, that link mind and body." Realizing the importance of her discoveries, and the heavy-hitting effects of emotions on a cellular level, can be paramount to not allowing toxic relationships to control your health and well-being.

If left to fester, overwhelming emotions can contribute to disease. Make a mental note of the following: the key to dealing with emotions that threaten to drown us is to release and express them without trying to stuff them deep inside. Let them go and give yourself a chance to move forward.

The power of both loving and unloving relationships must not be underestimated, as your body reflects this power in the status of your health. As Deepak Chopra states in his book, *Reinventing the Body, Resurrecting the Soul*, "Your immune system gets stronger or weaker in response to being in either a loving or unloving relationship." Reflect that truth in the relationships you allow in your life.

I know firsthand that relationships with family and friends are critical for our well-being. Unfortunately, in my case, it was the un-loving relationships that were my greatest teachers.

As you know, some relationships can be hazardous to our health. There is scientific evidence to support this, which can be found not only in Candace Pert's work, but also in the work of so many others. Personal relationships must be emotionally safe and allow one to ex-press their true self. It is vitally important that we feel free to be who we truly are.

Behind Closed Doors

What Terror the Eyes Can See

           ❝*Be with those who support your being.***❞**

– Rumi

The true value of a positive self-image became all too clear for me in my own life. Scenes of emotional abuse that tore away at my emo-tional stability became commonplace; oftentimes, they began with everyday activities, such as was the case for the following memory:

It was a beautiful, warm summer evening and the smell of the grill on the deck wafted its way to the kitchen. I was setting the table and straightening up, the evening news was on in the family room, and the voice of my son as he arrived home after a neighborhood game of kickball signaled it was time for dinner. He turned off the TV, washed his hands like any good athlete would, and slid into his chair at the kitchen table.

My husband had prepared pork chops on the grill, and they sat cooling on a platter. The two of us joined my son at the kitchen table and played out our tradition of discussing the favorite part of each of our days and what we were thankful for. It was a picture-perfect mo-ment, until the peace in the room evaporated in an eruption of food being slammed into the garbage bin.

You might be asking, "What could have shattered such a nice meal?" Well, my son had asked whether the meat was fully cooked. That's it. A simple health concern was apparently enough to warrant an explosive reaction.

I wish I could say that was an isolated incident, one that happened once and then never again. However, this scene would replay itself in one form or another many times over. Feelings of shock and fright became the norm in my life. Looking back, I realize the dangerous territory we were entering.

At the time, it was difficult to discern the destructive nature of such a hurtful and harmful relationship as it progressed slowly. And, a very common desire for people in situations like this, there was always hope that each outburst was just an isolated incident that wouldn't repeat itself.

That was wishful thinking. In situations like mine, taking a hard look at what happens behind closed doors is necessary to realize the severity of what was happening. This takes courage, and at that point in my life, I didn't seem to have enough.

The following pages are going to take into account some of the difficult challenges that came into my life. My relationship with my former husband was incredibly difficult for me and exacerbated many of my health challenges. The problems and explosions that lined our time together were—from my felt-experience—incredibly painful. But, through the pain, came waves and waves of gifts.

Finding the Courage to Take a Stand

It truly is a slow slide into this kind of madness. Even more dangerous is accepting an accusation that you, in fact, may have been the cause of this behavior. Certain words still ring in my ears - "It's your fault that I did this, because you (and your MS fatigue) are so hard to live with," or "If I wasn't forced to make dinner tonight (because you didn't have the energy to do it yourself) this never would have happened." Somehow, it always managed to be my fault.

Unfortunately, I started to believe that there was truth in these accusations. The incidents of emotional abuse continued to escalate, until they finally culminated in a situation that I consider myself lucky to have escaped alive.

The National Multiple Sclerosis Society, in its summer 2009 issue of *Momentum*, stated, "Abuse occurs at higher rates to people with disabling diseases, including MS." Domestic abuse is not limited to physical abuse, but also encompasses psychological abuse.

So what happened that caused me to fear for my life? I will share the details of that traumatic and terrifying day a little later in this wave. But for now, let me just say that it took a great deal of courage, and a considerable amount of inner maintenance, to finally get to the point where I was able to take a stand for myself. This allowed me to set boundaries and ultimately leave that decidedly unhealthy relationship.

Eventually, I came to realize that this was the most loving thing I could do for both of us. It is imperative to have relationships that empower us the majority of the time. In nearly all relationships, there will be little exceptions that come about. But when those exceptions become the rule, something needs to change. If we remain in these constricting relationships, we will lose out on precious energy that should be focused on living a life of excellence.

It made a huge difference in my inner life and for my emotional well-being to decide that I was no longer going to pay the price of my health by being in such an extremely unhealthy relationship. I chose to disengage and only wish I would have had the courage, and the understanding of how, to leave sooner.

Authentically Honoring Yourself

Think about it, if you are not kind and respectful to yourself, why should you expect others to treat you with that decency? It all begins with you, and again, you have more control over your life than you may give yourself credit for. Treat yourself well, and others will follow suit. Stop complaining and focusing on the negative situations in your life, and it will transform before your eyes.

Ekhart Tolle wrote a wonderful book called *The Power of Now*, and I had the pleasure of following him as Oprah introduced it to the world. In his book he states, "See if you can catch yourself complaining in either speech or thought, about a situation you find yourself in, what other people say or do, your surroundings, your life situation, and even the weather. See if you can catch yourself complaining—for to complain is always non-acceptance of what is and it invariably carries an unconscious negative charge."

These words struck a chord with me, as I found myself complaining a little too often. I considered myself a positive person, but after reading Ekhart's words, I realized there was an opportunity for me to stop sending these senseless negative charges out into the world.

Never accept being the victim. Either leave the situation, change it into something better, or accept it. Make it a practice to begin with the power of being in the present, and shift every complaining thought towards bringing harmony to your life. Again, you can do this by accepting the situation, changing it, or leaving it.

From the tough experiences I painfully navigated, I learned many important lessons. One that resonates is to do everything in your power to not squander your life. Be true to yourself and be authentic. Don't waste your time on things that don't have meaning to you and that fail to bring you joy. Being loved starts with learning to love yourself more.

Love yourself. You are worth every ounce of it.

A Tangled Web of Lies

My next life lesson is that secrets perpetuate unhealthy behavior patterns and allow dysfunction to continue. Had I not been such a private person, I believe that the unhealthy side of my marriage would not have been allowed to continue as it did for so many years.

My life evolved into a living hell, and I found myself tangled in a web of cover-ups and lies. My desire to protect my husband, reinforced by worries of pain and shame, forced me into a life where I feared his next inevitable outburst. When I finally went to my family to let them know of my plans to escape by getting a divorce, they were in shock and disbelief. This added even more pain to an already unbearable situation.

To the outside world, he appeared to be the father and husband of the year. In actuality, our family dynamics and relationships were quite the opposite. Normal in public, but deranged behind closed doors. My husband had become a monster in my life. And yet, there was more to come, so much more to come.

It was the early morning hours of a Saturday in August, just a few weeks after bringing home Teddy, our new Yorkie puppy. The house held a certain serenity that was accompanied by the beautiful feeling of freshness brought on by a brand new day. Tiny whimpers escaped from the kennel in the laundry room just off the kitchen. Precious music at first, but quickly progressing into a crescendo of more urgent pleas from our little two-pound puppy.

From Bad to Worse

Early as it was, we were still under the covers, the sun just barely peaking through the blinds. I woke to the sounds of Teddy, but also found myself with that all-too-familiar feeling of being hit by a truck, as often happens to those who experience the draining effects of a dis-ease. Getting out of bed did not seem like a good idea, but Teddy couldn't wait.

So I turned over and asked my husband if he would please let Teddy out. At first, there was silence. I asked again, and this time added the explanation of how I was not feeling well and would *really* appreciate it if he could help me by letting Teddy outside.

The grumbling began and steadily increased. It continued as he went down the steps and then suddenly, after a moment of peaceful silence, it escalated into a violent storm. Smash, crash, smash and crash! "Oh my God, what is going on!?" I cried out. Adrenalin took over, and within moments I found myself standing at the edge of the kitchen in shock and disbelief. My mind tried to process what I was seeing, and at the same time was giving me strong warning signals to stay back in order to protect myself.

There was my husband, standing over the dishwasher with the racks extended all the way out. In a violent rage he was working his way through the glasses one by one, lifting them above the rack and then smashing them back down. Glass was flying everywhere.

He was out of control; this rage was an all-time high. I saw my son out of the corner of my eye. He looked just as terrified as I am sure that I did. I quickly turned and ordered him to come with me upstairs where the two of us took shelter. I still remember that day as what it was—the beginning of the end. The permanent damage to the dishwasher reflected the lasting damage that had been done to our lives.

Seeing Light in The Dark of Tragedy

66A pearl is a beautiful thing that is produced by an injured life. It is the tear that results from the injury of the oyster. The treasure of our being in this world is also produced by an injured life. If we had not been wounded, if we had not been injured, then we will not produce the pearl.99

– Stephen Hoeller

Several years ago, I heard someone say, "If you let go of what won't be, you will be able to embrace all that can be." This is precisely what I found myself doing several years after that pivotal day in the kitchen.

After pleading with my then husband to get help and living through promise after broken promise, I realized that the only way forward was to move away from the tragedy. There was no longer any other choice in the matter and I needed to do what was necessary to protect me and my son. Looking back, it always amazes me how different I am now than I was back then and how I have been able to overcome the devastating effects left in the wake of those dark days.

Four Years Later

Now that you have seen a glimpse into the life I had, I am going to do something I never would have done back then; I am going to share a very personal part of my life. The following is my experience and the details I remember of the darkest day of my life.

April 27, 2009, is a day that will forever be engrained in my mind and a day I am grateful to have survived. This was the fateful day my then husband, who was still living in our home even though our divorce would be finalized by the end of May, came up the stairs from the basement with a gun in his hands.

We had planned for him to move out on the first of June, right after the divorce was finalized. We had been living in the same home for financial reasons, and I desperately tried to keep matters peaceful for the sake of our 16-year-old son. So much so, that I had proposed every-other-week family dinners on Sunday evenings. I felt that even though my husband and I were no longer together as a couple, we would still always be a family since we had a son together. In hindsight, it is hard for me to find a shred of common sense that indicates this could have ever worked. I already knew from prior experiences that when my husband got mad, things got ugly... really ugly.

It had been four long years since the dishwasher incident, but he never followed up on his promises to get the help he needed. It took me what seemed like forever to navigate my way out of that nightmare, but I was simply jumping from the frying pan into the fire.

The day began just like any other, but by mid-morning, it would prove to be anything but. My soon-to-be former husband called to let me know that he had once again been let go from his job. Understandably, I wasn't thrilled, as this was the third job he had been let go of in the last few years.

This time, he told me right away. With the previous job loss, he waited to tell me until I only had one day left to get my medication prescriptions filled under his company health insurance. Later, I found out that he had actually filled his own prescriptions weeks earlier without bothering with mine.

This was a huge reality check; he obviously did not care about my well-being, and when I sat face-to-face with this fact, a feeling of numbness set into my entire body. It was a wake-up call that told me that I had made the right decision in putting distance between us.

When he eventually came home after being let go from his job, we started to discuss financial matters. Specifically, we talked about what he was responsible for and what he needed to take care of in regards to the divorce. These were all things he was supposed to have done months earlier, but had not. I was concerned about his ability to obtain a credit card in his own name, which I had been urging him to do for some time. With him losing his job again, clearly time was of the essence.

Not What I Expected

This discussion broke out into an argument in the upstairs area of our two-story home. To my horror, I saw that familiar look in his eyes that deeply frightened me. That enraged, out-of-control look he had when he was about to snap.

Instinctively, I knew I needed to move away from him. At the same time, I realized his lack of follow through had put another obstacle in my way of breaking free of him. This lead to a flood of tears as I made my way down the stairs to the family room.

As I sat on the sofa, I heard him stomp down the stairs, turn the corner, and proceed down another flight of stairs into the basement. Thinking it was odd, I wondered why he had gone down there. Usually, he left in his car, not letting me know where he was going and leaving me to worry endlessly. I naively decided he must have gone down to the basement to get a coat he had in the downstairs closet.

Much to my disbelief, when he hurried back up the stairs, there was a gun in his hand. I sat on the sofa paralyzed with fear, shaking uncontrollably.

Thoughts were racing at warp speed through my mind. Should I hit the floor or stop breathing in order to not call attention to myself? No decision is a decision. I stayed put, frozen in fear.

Terror overtook my entire body. He turned, looked at me with glazed eyes and made sure I saw the gun. In that moment, I truly did not know if he was going to kill me or not. There was no one else in the world he was angrier with than me. I was abandoning him. His life had come crashing down in the past several months, and losing his job was the last straw.

Shaken to the Core of My Being

In my entire life, never had I felt the severity of the feelings in my body as I was experiencing in that moment. I saw my life flash before my eyes.

Many times I have been hard on myself and said things to myself like, "I should have escaped out the back door at the first sight of a problem," or "What was I doing not looking out for myself?" However, I have now come to a place of peace in knowing that I did the best I could in that terrifying situation. I am just incredibly grateful that I am still here to tell this story, and have another chance at life.

The one part that I remember so clearly is when he left through the laundry room and out to the garage. When I heard the laundry room door close, another split-second thought of terror struck - what if he just opened and shut the door, then remained in the laundry room waiting for me to follow so he could end it all there? Thankfully this was not the case, and the entire event ended without physical incident after I made the 911 call.

I am not exaggerating when I say that I was deeply, deeply shaken to the core. I felt like I had never, ever seen this person before in my life. He was a stranger I did not even recognize, despite the fact we had been husband and wife for many years, had a child, and had written so much of our history together.

I didn't know who this person was or what he was capable of. The words that best describe this event are *traumatic* and *terrifying*. I ended up suffering flashbacks and it took years before I could even talk about the incident without sobbing.

As devastating as that horrible day was, the years that followed have allowed me to see how much I have grown from it. I can honestly say I have found light through the darkness. This event is part of my life, but it doesn't define me, my life, or my future.

My life has gone on and the Divine has been so good to me. I can see the gift of that moment in teaching me how to be stronger than I have ever been. Most importantly, I know that I will never, ever, allow someone to subject me to emotional abuse again. I have now set healthy boundaries in all of my relationships, and I take full responsibility for how I am treated, by others and by myself.

Much good has come from that fateful day, and I am now able to stand back and see just how much richer my life has become. However, these are the end results of the ordeal. Before reaching the end of that path, there was more for me to heal and more for me to experience and learn about myself.

Standing Up for Myself

Regaining My Confidence

❝We are continually faced by great opportunities brilliantly disguised as insoluble problems.❞

–Lee Iacocca

The gun incident was bad enough, but afterwards, I found myself the subject of defamation and maligning attacks at the hand of the man who caused so much trauma in my life. I desperately wanted to move forward and allow the healing process to begin. I am a private person by nature, and this event brought about a great deal of shame for me.

So, as a result, I said nothing. From the start, I chose to keep this ugly secret buried, and made excuses to the neighbors who asked why the police were outside our home that fateful April day. I actually begged one of the officers to help me with a response, as I was deeply concerned for my son and his reputation with friends, both at school and his hockey team.

The police officer told me to say that I had accidentally pressed the panic button on our alarm system and, when this happens, they automatically respond and are required to check things out at the home. Although it was my deepest desire to put this whole chaotic mess behind us, my former husband had other plans. He waged a full-out attack, this time with sharpened words. He began to spread lies and misinformation to the people within our community.

What Will the Neighbors Think?

He distorted the truth by saying how I would "get everything in our divorce," "what a disgusting mother I had been," and how I had "turned my son against him." All of which were untrue. They were attempts from a hurt and wounded soul to hurt the one he thought had ruined his life. It is much easier to blame everyone else than to accept yourself as the problem.

By attacking me and making up falsehoods for the people in our community—mostly with other hockey parents—he was convincing in playing the role of the victim and made it a priority to convince them I was a horrible person. I confronted him about this and he responded with, "I have everyone in our city against you and for me."

Unfortunately, he continued this conduct and a considerable amount of damage was done to my reputation, as many of the hockey parents would not even look at, much less talk with me. I had not discussed his rage, nor the incidents mentioned above, to anyone. In my opinion, these were private matters and not to be discussed with the parents of my son's friends.

Given the fact that the majority of his friends were on the hockey team, my son was obviously aware of the rumors being spread about me. And, according to one hockey mom, he and I were a regular topic of conversation amongst most of the hockey families due to my former husband's conduct. Even so, I tried to protect him by not divulging any of his serious behavioral issues, even though he was making a spectacle of our family.

This would prove to be an extremely trying time for my son. I am so proud of how he made it through the tough times and how he still excelled in school and on the ice. In fact, at one point he even sent his dad emails encouraging him to turn his life around. On a hockey visit to Notre Dame, the head coach had given Andrew some great advice about school, hockey, and life in general, and he wanted to help his dad. It was incredible that my 16-year-old son was trying to get through to his father, but it was to no avail.

During this time, it took all I could muster to come up with the courage to finally stand up for myself. My attorney assured me that it was alright to talk about what happened to me, with regard to the gun incident, even though it was highly sensitive information.

So, with that blessing, I dug down as deep as I could and prayed for the courage it would take for me to stand up for myself, and to start telling people what really happened to me and my family. It was the hardest thing I have ever done, mainly because it was difficult to find people that were willing to sit down and listen. Once someone has made up their mind, it can be incredibly difficult to show them your truth.

Mending Fences

I began with my neighbors, as they had not been under the influence of my former husband's harsh lies. At the time, I was unable to tell my story without sobbing, but I knew this is what I needed to do. From there, I talked with one mom in the hockey community who was not as outwardly judgmental towards me and whom I thought would at least give me a chance to explain.

Slowly but surely, it got a little easier to discuss my recent past with each person I talked to. The gut wrenching feeling of being shunned was lifted as my truth was put out into the world. It was freeing beyond measure to finally find my voice and stand up for my son and I.

Eventually, I began regaining my confidence, which had been gone for a very long time. Even though I knew that there were going to be those who were already convinced by my former husband's campaign against me, I no longer cared about what people thought. For me, it was more about being able to find my certainty and my voice again!

The positive outcome is that I am now able to see that even in difficult challenges, there is good. In fact, I now know that good reigns supreme! All of these challenges have helped me strengthen my voice, find my words, and set boundaries that I expect to be respected. We must always remember that we do not need to change anyone else, nor is it up to us to do so. We shouldn't get frustrated, because we always have other options. If I am not being treated in the manner I would like, then I always have the right to remove myself from the relationship; this is where my true power lies. Only in recent years have I purposely chosen to remove myself from negative opinions, participation, and drama, but what a difference it has made!

These days, I receive my physical, emotional, and spiritual healing in so many life-giving ways. While it has taken me years and various challenges to become the person I am now, I am in a better position to help others facing these same challenges. This is my pot of gold at the end of the rainbow! This is what makes all of those experiences worth the pain.

As I am sure you are aware of by now, I have come to understand that the mind has the ability to shape the health of the body. When challenges come to us, ones like the challenges we have covered so far, the best way to respond is to keep asking yourself this all-important question - "How can I use this situation for the next best version of me, and how do I use this for good in the next phase, or chapters, of my own life?"

Sharing What Is in My Heart

❝ The body never lies—it says what words cannot. ❞

– Martha Graham

For me, helping others is that next phase of my life. I have been so fortunate to have found a perfect avenue to do so. It is kind of funny how life works, isn't it? More than anything else, we need to stay positive.

I am grateful for the opportunity to now be speaking and coaching others on how to live a life of health, well-being, abundance, and excellence; this is what I like to call a life of full-spectrum wealth. For instance, several years ago, I was asked to be a guest speaker at a patient education meeting put on by a neurologist at the highly regarded Minneapolis Clinic of Neurology.

It was an event sponsored by several pharmaceutical companies for their patients. I was brought in to speak on the benefits of massage as it related to healing injection-site reactions. At the time, I had been giving myself every-other-day injections for many years, and had struggled with injection-site reactions from the beginning. My skin wasn't healing and the damage from years of injections threatened my ability to continue taking the medication. That was scary, as I felt not being on the medication could prove to be devastating to my future prognosis.

Feeling frustrated and anxious, as I had tried everything suggested to me over the years but found no relief, I started to think there was no answer. That was until a nurse evaluated my skin and prescribed what I hoped would enable me to continue the injections. She suggested a "full-court press" of massage and physical therapy, and I am pleased to report that it proved to be a huge success. And, wouldn't you believe, that it wasn't such a bad "prescription!" Specifically, the massage part was incredibly beneficial and enjoyable!

This is exactly the kind of information that needs to be shared with other patients so they can be aware of inspiring solutions to challenging problems like injection-site reactions. And I was now in a position to be one of the people spreading this knowledge, handing out this hope for a better life.

So, on a beautifully sunny—but chilly—February day, the meeting began at the neurology clinic. It kicked off with introductions and the agenda, which would follow lunch. My massage therapist, who had done such wonders for me, was there along with the original nurse who had recommended massage as a therapy option. Needless to say, I was in good company!

The three of us took turns speaking about the success of this therapy from three unique perspectives. When it came to my turn, I shared how grateful I was to have found such a miraculous solution.

By incorporating regular massage treatments into my routine, the healing of my skin had gone from an eight-month recovery process after each injection to finding relief after only two months' time! I think we can all agree that those results are incredible.

The massage therapist spoke about the techniques he used, along with recommendations for frequency and duration of the massages. The nurse focused on the importance of finding a solution to injection-site reactions, ensuring that the patient can continue to take the necessary medications. All in all, the meeting was a big success and, at the end, I found there was a line of people waiting to talk with me.

To see so many patients wanting to connect afterwards was humbling, but I knew exactly what they were going through. Our paths may have been slightly different, but in many ways they were exactly the same. And, wouldn't you know, many of them had questions completely unrelated to massage therapy and injection sites!

My main takeaway was that there is a huge need for people to connect and learn from each other in a positive emotional setting. That need calls for an environment that focuses on what each of us can do to not only thrive, but live a life of excellence. This is my story.

There was one woman in particular who came up to me after the meeting; she was newly diagnosed, and we talked about self-care and loving yourself. I remember how she was so frightened to start the harsh injections, and was thinking of putting them off for now. I told her if there was one thing she should leave with from the talk, it was to have hope for a bright future. I explained that I am a firm believer in doing everything you can for yourself, which includes practicing all components of self-care, including your mind, body, and spirit.

For example, I enjoy the many benefits of taking a bath. On the evenings that I gave myself an injection, I would usually treat myself to a luxurious bath. The relaxation of the warm water genuinely helped the injection go better. Different techniques and self-care practices can work together to increase your overall well-being.

Approaching Wellness from All Angles

This meeting made a significant impression on me. It is what made me ultimately realize the tremendous need to share all of the information that I had discovered during the many years I had been living with my dis-ease. We are all handed challenges, each of them adding some degree of difficulty to our lives. In this way, they take away the ease of a stress-free life. And thus, they become our very own dis-ease. Some of these are actual physical conditions, but others may take shape as different roadblocks along our paths. My primary challenges or dis-ease have revolved around my health, yours may be with your relationships or your finances. Whatever your dis-ease may be, it does not define you.

I truly believe in approaching health from all angles, using the best of Western, Eastern, and integrative medicine. In fact, I am enthusiastic about the ways they can so beautifully complement one another.

For me in particular, my #1 health priority is maximizing energy. Since my energy is oftentimes compromised and is a scarce commodity, I am always searching for new things to try. These have come in the forms of medications, meditation, exercise, positive thought processes, visualization, energy management techniques, and many others.

As we continue on our journey together, I will touch on each of these areas to give you a variety of options to choose from, and to help you find what strategies work best for you.

Shell 1: It's All About Me!

❝I have learned that the greater part of our misery or unhappiness is determined not by our circumstance but by our disposition.❞

– Martha Washington

Self-worth is primarily defined by who we believe ourselves to be, and not about how someone else might see us. It is about our relationships with ourselves, our love turned inward, and how brightly we allow our light to shine. It is incredibly refreshing to know that we do not need approval from anyone else to feel like we are worthy of love. For years, I looked outside myself for self-worth, and it left me feeling lonely and unworthy.

With those certainties in place, I think most of us can agree that connecting with others is a primary goal in our lives. For some of us it comes naturally, but for others, it takes a little bit more effort. Regardless of the ease or difficulty that we have forming relationships, it is an important aspect and contributor to our well-being. But, and this is a major contingency, this is true *only if these relationships are healthy*.

We are wired to connect with others, and isolation can lead to some serious health issues, both physical and mental. The primary litmus test when taking a look at whether our relationships are healthy for us is to determine if they fill us up, or if the relationship is draining us instead.

But what will people think of me?

This is a big one for many people. Yes, it is important to be kind, generous, humble, loving, truthful, full of integrity, and to have other noble characteristics. But, we must be true to ourselves first and place our initial concern on how we view ourselves, asking questions such as, "What do I think of me?" There is no way to please everyone, and it is simply not possible to meet everyone else's expectations, so don't waste your precious time and energy trying to do this. Instead, strive to make "you" proud of the person you decide to be!

If there is a relationship in our lives that leaves us feeling drained, we may need to let go for the sake of our health. On the other hand, if we feel brighter and lighter after interactions with certain people, these are the relationships we want to nurture and cultivate. The positive energy we receive from healthy relationships is imperative to our health and well-being.

How brightly will I allow my light to shine?

The answer to this question is entirely up to you, but why would you want to limit yourself? Some may not be comfortable in what they consider to be the spotlight. Others may be concerned that if they shine, others will be diminished in some way. There are as many varied reasons as there are people, but what I have to say is this - let your brightness shine brilliantly for all to see. That way you can help others through leading by example and allowing them to let their own brilliance out as well. I believe there is no real service to others if we keep our gifts hidden in the shadows.

My natural tendency is to be sensitive and connect with others on a heart level, and in hindsight I see that for a long time that sensitive nature was suppressed. I too kept my gifts hidden away.

The emotional loneliness I experienced within my marriage was a result of not realizing my self-worth. This kind of relationship is no longer an option in my life and is strictly non-negotiable. I have also come to realize that I can improve my meaningful relationships by simply expressing what is in my heart. Let your voice ring true and your light shine bright.

Shell 2: My Life's Thermostat

No one makes you feel inferior without your consent.
— Eleanor Roosevelt

Let's turn up the heat! Imagine that we have a thermostat in our home and the temperature is set at 72 degrees. Now, if it gets colder outside, the furnace is going to kick in, and when it gets warmer outside, the air conditioner is going to bring the temperature right back to the 72 degrees we set. Our self-worth is much the same. We have a set point for what we feel we deserve and who we believe we are.

How do I know what my set point is set at?

Take a look at your current results as they are a great barometer for your current setting. What has your life looked like for the past 12 months? Remember, results never lie, and they are a looking glass into what is in store for the days ahead… unless you reset your self-worth thermostat! Only then can you truly welcome in more health, love, wealth, and abundance in all areas of your life. When realization meets decision, you give yourself opportunity to improve your life and change the circumstances you find yourself in.

If we want more warmth in our lives, we need to turn up the heat. In order to do that, we must raise our internal self-worth thermostat, turning up the amount of good we allow into our lives.

The bottom line is that we set the controls. No one else can raise our thermostats for us. Let's say we have it set a comfortable 72 degrees, and somebody tells us, "Oh my gosh, this was great," or "You are wonderful!" Even with these nice compliments, our set point will eventually return right back to where we feel most comfortable.

130

Sure, we may take these compliments and say "Thank you" or "That's great," but deep down we are going to still believe what we have already decided to be true about ourselves. This is where the important "inner work" comes into play. Again, we may begin to discount these compliments—or all of the good things being said about us—because deep down, our subconscious thoughts stay true to what we already believe about ourselves. And, if how we see ourselves has a negative connotation, all of the compliments in the world wouldn't be enough to change us.

What's wrong with feeling comfortable?

Nothing, unless what you really want is a life of excellence that is filled with vibrant health and well-being, rich relationships, and freedom of time and money! And remember the amazing added benefit of maintaining your youthfulness! Being comfortable keeps us in line with the status quo. As spiritual beings taking part in this human experience, we are hardwired to want to bring more and more into our lives. If you have that small voice whispering in your ear that suggests there might be more for you to do, be, or have, then try to make a habit of letting yourself be uncomfortable here and there. Only then will you let that uncomfortable feeling stretch and cause you to grow. The alternative is that you are not growing, and from my experience, things that are not growing are dying.

No one said we had to keep our lives set at a comfortable 72 degrees. But then again, many people are just seeking out a life of contentment. However, in order to bring more warmth into our lives, we may need to turn up the heat to grow into the person we are meant to be.

As is the case for most anything else, learning something new can cause us to feel out of sorts and unsure of ourselves. But, with practice, we feel more aware and capable. Learn to be uncomfortable, and soon enough the things that were uncomfortable before will start to feel comfortable again, starting a beautiful cycle that pushes us to new challenges that shake up our comfort once again.

131

Shell 3: The Myth of Perfectionism

❝We cannot think of being acceptable to others until we have first proven acceptable to ourselves.❞

– Malcolm X

There is no such thing as perfectionism; it simply does not exist. You see, no one is perfect. We are simply doing the best we can with what we have. This is a self-critical piece, and I have learned to create a no-judgment zone for myself and others.

Why wouldn't I strive to be the best I can be?

Please don't get me wrong, you should *always* strive to be the best you can be. Just avoid overdoing it by chasing perfection. Not only will that fail to get you anywhere fast, it will also take a huge toll on your body's health and well-being. Perfectionism is a myth and not attainable, so instead, try to do your best at all times, and strive to be a great example for others.

I was a perfectionist, or strived to be, and this thinking caused me to focus on the one or two things that weren't quite perfect. So, instead of focusing on the myriad of moments that went so very well, my focus was instead on those things that did not go quite as well as I would have liked. Clearly there was an unhealthiness to this relentless pursuit of perfection.

In the end, we need to bring our focus back to the things that went well. These days, I require myself to spend time meditating on and expressing gratitude for all the things that go right. In the past, I wasn't doing this, and it revealed itself in both my well-being and in my body. Learn from your mistakes, let them go, and then shift back to thinking about all the things that have and continue to go well. Shift your focus onto the things that you would love and let them come to you. It is a practice, much like anything else. Take the time to make it your own reality and experience the amazing effects on your mind and body!

Shell 4: The Gentle Practice

❝Never forget that once upon a time, in an unguarded moment, you recognized yourself as a friend.❞

Elizabeth Gilbert

Be gentle on yourself. That has been a wonderful practice for me and I hope that it does the same for you! Most of us tend to be far too hard on ourselves.

One thing that has helped me to be more gentle on myself is to watch mentors and others whom I hold in high regard. When something does not go well for them, they handle it with a simple, "That was okay, we will learn from it and do better next time." They recover from what went wrong, say a quick "Oh well," and move right along. This is one of the very best things about this practice - it is basically a free pass. You can move past what went wrong and refuse to let it influence whatever comes next.

Why am I so hard on myself?

This question comes right back to the subject of self-worth. If I am feeling good about who I am and hold myself in high regard, then I would never dream of shredding myself over something that did not go as I would have liked or as I had planned. Taking this one small step further, if I hold myself in high regard, I make it easy to extend this same gentleness to others when they are not perfect. I believe the best way to handle these circumstances is to come from a place of love and understanding. Again, we are all doing the best we can with what we have, so give yourself credit and share this gift whenever and wherever you can.

Try and remember that it is not just the recovery on the outside that matters, but also the recovery on the inside. I watch my mentors often, and I can see that they refuse to hold onto these glitches and beat themselves up. They move through it gracefully, let it go, and move on. Don't be discouraged if you find this to be harder than it seems on paper. While it is something I try to do myself, moving through the inner dismay and turmoil has challenged me extensively in the past. Put in the practice to be more gentle with yourself. Just remember, Rome wasn't built in a day.

What is the best way to move through mistakes gracefully?

Move purposefully with love and compassion for yourself and for others. We all make mistakes from time to time. Once again, no one is perfect, and we should never try to be. Use humor and laugh it off. Most times, a simple laugh is all that is needed as long as you make a note and continue to improve in the future. Others will understand, and if they don't, then it is clear that they need to work on having more love and compassion themselves.

In the end, what will have the greatest impact and improvement upon your health and well-being is adding more love and compassion to your life. Give more of it to yourself, and pass the wealth along to others. There can never be too much of this love, and it will never, ever lead you astray. So, increase the dosage on this vital daily prescription in order to lead a happier and healthier life. You will definitely be glad you did.

Grains of Sand:

In review, let's quickly go over the highlights from this wave on self-worth. The biggest takeaway must be that, no matter what, you should be gentle on yourself and on others. Even in the face of danger and tragedies, there can be learning opportunities and blessings.

For me, unfortunately, I did not listen to the gentle warning whispers about what was happening in my personal life. It was not until the hammer came slamming down that I was shoved into action. But in looking back, I am pleased to see that these horrible events—events that endangered my life—were in fact turning points that propelled me into the life I was always meant to have.

* Relationships can be healthy and unhealthy
* It takes courage to make a stand
* We must always choose to honor ourselves
* Love and compassion heal all wounds

It is with these points that we can now close this wave. For just a moment, take a look at your own life and relationships and try to pinpoint areas where there may be some discord or where improvements can be made. Have an honest "self-check" of your current results and plan changes for those areas that are less than ideal. Remember, it is your life, so make the most of it at all times!

WAVE FIVE
GRACE

From my experience, I have come to view grace and forgiveness as interchangeable words. In grace, we find a medicine that is extended to ourselves for ourselves, and also spreads to others for their benefit. To have complete dominion over the health and well-being of our bodies, we must develop a refined practice of forgiveness. Intellectually, we might understand the concept of forgiveness, and we may even think we are practicing it, but there are many layers—and even greater depths—to be explored in an effort to experience true release through grace. If we hold tight to unhealthy experiences and fail to forgive as we should, the toxins held in our cells are allowed to build up. It is vital that we release these toxins from our bodies in order to live a life of vibrant health. We owe it to ourselves to forgive and spread grace in everything we do.

A Different Kind of Medicine

In This Chapter

* Establishing boundaries and keeping the master key
* Healing love that brings clarity and forgiveness

"Love said, there is nothing that is not me. Be silent."

– Rumi

We have arrived at one of my favorite topics—grace! From my experiences, I have come to understand that grace is synonymous with forgiveness. Grace is the forgiveness we extend to ourselves and to everyone else we come in contact with. Forgiveness is vital for our health and well-being. After all, it has a major effect on what our inner pharmacy dispenses each and every day!

Being Master of My Own Body

At first blush, one might see the phrase "being the master of my own body" as an unfounded attempt to exert control. After all, it insinuates a dynamic where one part plays the master while the other plays the servant; this is likely to go against many of our instincts for equal footing. However, what I am presenting here is the idea that we must have dominion over the *health and well-being* of our own bodies. One of the easiest and most effective ways to do this is by embracing forgiveness.

Forgiveness is often misunderstood; it is *not* a golden opportunity for others to take advantage of your good nature. Instead, it is primarily a call for love. Remember this even when your forgiveness is being turned inward, since forgiveness and self-love go hand in hand.

138

Many do not understand the gift of forgiveness or what it truly entails. One school of thought teaches that we ought to "forgive and forget" or "turn the other cheek." In other words, these mentalities ask that we pretend a situation does not hurt or never happened. Intellectually, we may think we know all about forgiveness, and we may even think we are actively practicing it, but there are many layers to experiencing a true release through forgiveness and grace.

I invite you, for the sake of your health, to open yourself to releasing the upsets you may be holding tightly. If we are choosing not to forgive, the toxins of these negative emotions and feelings are held in our cells. It is imperative that we release these toxins in order to live a life of vibrant health. If we do not let them go gracefully, it is a dark road they lead us down. Take an early detour and use grace as your GPS to redirect your course.

The Key to Unlock the Code

Healing Down to The Cellular Level

‟A physician once said, the best medicine is love. Someone asked, what if it doesn't work? He said, increase the dosage.”

– Unknown

What does "healing down to the cellular level" mean exactly? Well, we have already seen the incredible power of our thoughts and their ability to help or harm our physical bodies, but there is more to these words than first meets the eye. It was an enormous blessing when I first discovered science-based concepts that clearly showed the body's ability to heal itself. Knowing that the beliefs I was exploring were backed by scientific evidence made it that much easier for me to further open my mind to the ability of healing ourselves through self-love.

Already aware that our minds are powerful beyond measure, I also came to understand that our thoughts directly affect the state of our physical bodies. But, what I discovered next fully supported this understanding with hard scientific proof. What I am referring to is quantum biology, which I hope you find as fascinating as I do!

In his book, *The Biology of Belief*, Dr. Bruce Lipton states, "emotions of a higher vibration, such as love, over-power the negative programming." Mind-blowing concepts such as this one have expanded my understanding that anything is possible!

The following is taken from the inside jacket of Lipton's book:

"The Biology of Belief is groundbreaking work in the field of new biology. Author Bruce H. Lipton, Ph.D., is a former medical school professor and research scientist. His experiments, and those of other leading-edge scientists, have examined the mechanisms by which cells receive and process information in great detail. The implications of this research radically change our understanding of life. It shows that genes and DNA do not control our biology; but instead, DNA is controlled by signals from outside the cell, including the energetic messages emanating from our positive and negative thoughts. This profoundly hopeful synthesis of the latest and best research in cell biology and quantum physics is being hailed as a major breakthrough, showing that our bodies can be changed as we retrain our thinking."

The fact that DNA, so integral to making our physical selves who we are, becomes tight with fear and relaxes with love carries a weight that feels so true on the deepest level. When I get in touch with how my body feels when experiencing love and fear, it lines up perfectly with the respective feelings of relaxation or tightness.

Realizing this, I felt—for the first time in my life—that I had found the master key to my own vibrant health and well-being. My inner instincts told me that this is precisely how we can best cope with pain and dis-ease.

I was simply blown away to have my suspicions so assuredly confirmed! Once I discovered how science could back up my beliefs, I also found there are others out there doing the same type of work as Dr. Lipton. According to Dr. Mehmet Oz, "Energy Medicine is the future of medicine." After reading this, I knew that I had already realized and started to unlock this statement of truth in my own life.

More Than Just Positive Thinking

In Dr. Lipton's powerful book, one of the first things that caught my eye was when he said, "It is not gene-directed hormones and neurotransmitters that control our bodies and our minds, our beliefs control our bodies, our minds, and thus our lives. Oh ye of little belief!" He follows this with the following:

"Positive thoughts have a profound effect on behavior and genes, but only when they are in harmony with subconscious programming.

Negative thoughts have an equally powerful effect. When we recognize how these positive and negative beliefs control our biology, we can use this knowledge to create lives filled with health and happiness."

This way of thinking is key to unlocking the code to our health and well-being. The joy I felt after discovering these truths was confirmation that I was personally experiencing their existence.

The environment we provide for our bodies, reaching down to the cellular level, determines whether health will prevail. When we have a toxic environment filled with negative emotions, feelings, and fear, not to mention all of the toxins in our food and the air we breathe, our bodies will falter. And yet, when we provide a healthy environment for ourselves, one spanning all levels, our bodies thrive. A healthy physical and mental environment also promotes our ability to maintain youthfulness as our inner pharmacy releases beautiful chemicals that every cell in our body can bathe in.

All of this seems like common sense and so simple in theory. Yet, when we apply these principles and recognize how our beliefs and lives can so easily get in the way, we start to see their complex nature.

No Need to Cling to Past Beliefs

The great news is that Dr. Lipton also indicates that when he adjusted the "sick" cells, they were able to revitalize themselves. This gives extra power to the certainty that our cells are shaped by the environment we find ourselves in.

Dr. Lipton confirms this by noting, "Biological behavior can be controlled by invisible forces, including thought, as well as it can be controlled by physical molecules like penicillin, a fact that provides the scientific underpinning for pharmaceutical-free energy medicine." My hope is that with this wonderful information in hand, we will all understand the power we have over how our genes express themselves. Now that is pretty exciting!

We have the strength to affect the outcomes of our health; our own internal resources have such immense power. A power that has already been proven with the placebo effect, and yet, some doctors still brush these truths aside. I know that might seem hard to believe, especially with all of the scientific evidence out there, but many doctors still cling to beliefs that are quickly becoming outdated.

The astonishing power of the placebo effect was documented in a 2002 Baylor School of Medicine Study, which was published in the New England Journal of Medicine. It evaluated surgery for patients with severe and debilitating knee pain. Patients were divided into three groups: in the first group, the damaged cartilage was shaved; the second group received a flushing of the knee joint; and the third group received a "fake" surgery. The results were shocking and clearly substantiated the enormous power of belief. In this study, the placebo group improved just as much as the other two groups! You see, when our mind changes—and our beliefs change along with it—it absolutely affects our physical bodies as well.

The Biology of Belief also takes a look at how the laws of quantum physics—everything is energy—have been practiced for thousands of years. Dr. Lipton states, "For thousands of years, and long before Western scientists discovered the laws of quantum physics, Asians have honored energy as the principle factor contributing to health and well-being." All of this powerful information made me take a more serious look at how I was spending my own energy. It gave me the go-ahead to pay attention to the thoughts that fed off my energy, allowing me to monitor them carefully.

So, in the words of my mentor and dear friend, Mary Morrissey, the most important skill to master is to "notice what you are noticing." It is only then that we can make the necessary changes in our thinking patterns and, therefore, our lives.

Breaking Patterns of Worry

Shocked at my own findings, it was apparent how many events in my life had centered around worry and fear. Considering the positive person I felt I was, it was surprising to notice just how much I worried about *everything*. In fact, these dangerous thoughts were a constant pattern bombarding my mind. They served only to bathe my cells in negative energy and create a toxic environment for my body.

One of the most profound statements in Lipton's book says, "The fact is that harnessing the power of your mind can be more effective than the drugs you have been programmed to believe you need... energy is a more efficient means of affecting matter than chemicals." I always knew that I had a powerful mind, but Dr. Lipton was adding credence to my belief that our minds can surpass the effects of dangerous chemicals.

Our challenge now is dealing with both a conscious mind and a subconscious mind, the latter being infinitely more powerful. In other words, as a child, if you heard statements such as, "You are stupid" or "You will never amount to anything," these ideas are then programmed into your subconscious mind and will restrict many of your efforts in life. Fortunately, the subconscious mind is programmable, and there are methods to help reprogram it. Two wonderful methods I personally use for reprograming are tapping and theta healing.

Please note that what Dr. Lipton is sharing with us is far more than just positive thinking. He says we must shift our mind's energy towards life-generating thoughts that promote healing energy, leaving behind energy-draining thoughts of all kinds. Remember, these thoughts only serve to create toxic environments that make true health impossible.

This is precisely what my coaching program, OCEANS OF WELLNESS˚ - A Fountain of Youth, is all about. It is the "how" behind making these results a reality in our lives. We will take a closer look at some of the amazing tools for transformation I use with my clients over the coming pages, but first I want to emphasize this truth - no matter what path we decide to take regarding our beliefs, we must let go of unfounded fears and create our own change. You are a force to be reckoned with, don't ever forget it!

We must shift our lives towards growth, and the best growth amplifier I have found is grace and forgiveness. Why? Because they bring us to the vibration of love, what I believe to be the most powerful force in the universe.

Establishing Healthy Boundaries

Self-worth has everything to do with how you love, respect, and treat yourself. And by means of this we teach people how to treat us.

– Kathryn Ford

All of these newly discovered resources came face to face with what I had known all along. My emotions can, and do, affect my physical body. For me, the hard evidence of this was noticing what symptoms showed up in my own body. After particularly disturbing events and confrontations that seemed to strike from out of the blue, I could clearly see that I was left with a wake of emotions spreading throughout my body.

I could feel the after effects as I lay in bed scanning myself from head to toe. In doing so, I was trying to get in touch with the negative, destructive pain my body was left to deal with. Initially, it was easy to see that my head was aching, my chest was tight, and my abdominal area felt sick.

When I made this conscious effort to check in with my body, it became obvious that unhealthy tolls had been taken on my physical being by these negative events. And, remember, this was only what I noticed on a surface level, so just imagine what my *cells* were subjected to as a result of my system processing these emotional reactions.

It was after one such event that I knew in my heart I had to change the way I was dealing with these types of situations. I could no longer afford to simply leave and allow the other person's anger, frustration, or foul emotions to linger. Once I allowed these emotions to enter my body, the toxicity was free to run wild.

My emotions were becoming toxic inside of my body. To counteract this, the first thing I learned to do was to take deep breaths and relax as a way of clearing these dark energies. As it turned out, I still had restless nights, which included some old symptoms of MS/NMO. The most pronounced were pains in my hip and tingling sensations throughout my right leg. However, most alarming was when I woke up in the middle of the night and my entire right leg and foot were numb. I knew it was no coincidence that this physical manifestation was presenting itself after emotionally traumatic events.

Now, I no longer take any of these negative emotions with me. I address them and then leave them where they originated and where they belong. For instance, I may state, "Please stop and listen to me," in the middle of a confrontation where I am not being heard. This will usually get the other person's attention and allow room for discussion, but if not, I know I must remove myself from the situation. Knowing that I pushed for peace is in itself a gift to my health.

Physical Effects of Emotions

I also practice this strategy when it comes to inappropriate behaviors. I know if I let them continue, they will only hurt me. I used to swallow those negative emotions, which ultimately led to subsequent attacks on my well-being and health. But now, if I am being spoken to inappropriately, I am quick to stand up for myself, find my voice, and simply state, "Please don't speak to me that way."

It feels good to express the love and respect for myself that I deserve, as well as expecting others to respect my boundaries. I have reclaimed my voice and am so glad that I did. Hopefully, for those of you who have also felt your voice slip away, you can put these practices into place and revel in the reclaiming of your own voice. I have found, and I am sure that you will as well, that our health depends on expressing ourselves properly.

After situations like these, I will take the very next time I meditate to connect with my "God Self" and make a conscious effort to heal. I set my intention, envision myself enveloped in a sparkling beautiful light of love, and say to myself what I heard Wayne Dyer suggest, "I Am That I Am, I Am That I Am." By doing this, I feel at one with the Divine, who is my source.

For many years, it has been my experience to see a beautiful purple light when I have made that connection with the Divine during meditation. As soon as this happens, I begin mixing in the "I Am That I Am" with the recognition that "I am perfect health." I say these mantras over and over throughout my meditation and quietly drift off to sleep. I connect with my God Self and become the master of my body. I have come to realize that emotional issues can be more draining than physical events.

I must always remember to be vigilant of the energy that I allow into my space and remember that I have control over how I respond to a negative flow. The reality that I always have alternative choices and do not need to tolerate inappropriate behavior is wildly comforting.

In extreme situations—as a last resort—I know that I can always move away from destructive energy as a matter of self-defense. Many of my own experiences have made it loud and clear that I must protect my health through enforcing healthy boundaries and healthy reactions to everyday events. At the end of the day, I am the one responsible for what I let in and for allowing negativity to affect me.

146

Regeneration of a Solid Foundation

My definition of healing has come to include the word "balance." This has certainly shown up in my embracing of Chinese and Oriental Medicine. These Asian influences help me place the focus on achieving balance in everything I do.

One way to see the effects of balance on our physical being is to look at the outside. Our skin is a window into the state of our health, making me particularly cautious when the severity of my skin issues increased after the NMO infusions. I knew on some level that this was a sign of something much deeper and more profound. And, finally, I discovered an answer to the mystery.

This revelation was one of balance, harmony, and serenity, the three foundations of peace and joy. Balance became my focus once I realized that my body could not tolerate the infusion treatments.

One of my first holistic practitioners practiced traditional Chinese Medicine along with other modalities, such as acupuncture. In support of my new realization, he declared that the three months following my initial appointment were going to be a rebirthing period for me.

Right from the beginning of this process, it felt as though I had been put in a cocoon. I hadn't experienced the deep napping and restful sleep that followed since I was a little girl. This embarking marked the beginning of a deeper and more complete transformation. I was much like a caterpillar when they first move into their cocoon as a temporary resting place. It was deeply transforming, all the way down to the cellular level. The new me was emerging.

There were both exciting and scary feelings during those three months, since I knew I would have new experiences throughout this unfolding process, and I could only imagine what was going to happen next. In order to find myself, I kept reiterating a need to be open and receptive to all of the gifts that were unfolding before me.

The new me exercises my power by doing what I can instead of trying to change the other person. I use my voice, my heart, and my spirit. At times, this means that I must exercise the right to remove an individual from my life if they continue as a toxic influence.

Instead of remaining silent and feeling like there is nothing else I can do if others refuse to change, I use my newfound voice. I have established boundaries to ensure that I am loved and respected.

In their book, *You Are God*, authors Michael Love and Judy Johnston plainly say, "Allow yourself to love you. Allow yourself to love everything around you. If you don't like something that's already there, move away from it. If what you don't like is inside you, then let it go, knowing you will only have internal conflict until it has been released." Precious advice, indeed.

Unconventional Wisdom

Reconnecting to The Essence of You

66*You yourself, as much as anybody in the entire universe, deserve your love and affection.*99

– Buddha

The third appointment with my wonderful practitioner took place three months after the initial consultation. At this point, I was two-thirds of the way through the rebirthing process, and had already noticed significant improvement in my right leg. Walking started to feel more normal, which was a miracle by itself. My decreased difficulties with walking and the strength that was returning to my leg showed me that the new approach was working. I had learned to live with my symptoms for almost twenty years, and it only took a few short months to make them fade. My progress was significant and rapid.

My body had forgotten how to be well and needed to relearn, all the way down to the cellular level. I am so grateful that I found a practitioner who knew just what to do to help my body progress through this process gracefully.

Within three months, my remedies and treatments were reduced, and I was told to schedule my next check-up in two months' time. Obviously, progress had begun, and we were both pleased with the results. Actually, that is an understatement. I was *thrilled* with the results! Here are some of the notes I took from our appointments:

* Laughter is the best medicine.
* There are toxins in your body and your immune system is under constant attack.
* I have had a great deal of emotional attacks throughout my life—that is one half of the equation. The other half, the physical side, is seen through the self-attack of the autoimmune dis-ease.

My holistic practitioner also performed acupuncture treatments to aid my digestion. It was the first time I had ever experienced this modality and found it to be both powerful and enlightening. I could feel sensations of energy in my body, my abdominal region began to make noise, and then I started to feel a strange sensation in my left eye.

More Control Than Thought Possible

With this new feeling taking place, I asked, "Is it possible that I would be feeling something in my left eye from this?" My practitioner looked at me and said, "Yes, because it is along the same meridian. You are a very sensitive person to be able to feel that, and this is just your first time."

He then asked me to meditate on my digestive system and thank it for ridding my body of all waste and toxins. In addition, I should be sure to send it waves of love.

My holistic practitioner also reaffirmed and strongly encouraged me to continue with my new daily practice of chakra clearing, along with my evening meditations. I can't tell you just how incredible it feels to focus completely on wellness instead of setting my attention on fighting sickness!

What I realized after the "talking to my intestines" session, is that I have control over my body. This, coupled with a few other healing techniques I was shown, have led to a substantial reduction of intestinal problems. They really work.

I found affirmation in what I already knew to be true: the communication between my mind and my body is always there and ready for me to direct. I began to see in action how my mind and body are one, and how holistic and complimentary medicine could act as the catalyst to my healing.

My fourth appointment was nothing short of an epiphany. It was centered around new developments in my life, namely speaking my truth and no longer allowing for emotional suppression. Instead, I was learning how to use my voice with statements such as, "Please don't speak to me that way..." when I experienced disrespectful speech from others.

Early in the process, I would simply say, "I am working on finding my voice and connecting my feelings to words, so please give me a minute to get centered and to find the words for what I am feeling." I found with practice it gets easier to attach exact and precise words to match the feelings in my heart. Start simple and work your way up until you can properly verbalize the emotions you have coursing through you.

All of the relationships in my life have benefitted from this healthy and direct communication. Likewise, this style is completely in harmony with how I feel about honoring others in a kind manner. This is one of the shifts that have had a life-changing impact on my entire life!

Healing Miracles and Forgiveness

66*When you forgive, you in no way change the past, but you sure do change the future.*99

– Bernard Meltzer

Dr. Wayne Dyer was frequently asked to speak at Unity churches across the country, so I decided to visit the local congregation in Minneapolis. It was nice to finally visit this church, which emphasizes that no matter where you are on your spiritual journey, you are always welcome. This church practices many of the principles that Dr. Dyer teaches, and I have found that each service has been quite valuable.

On one Sunday morning, several local healers that participate in the church's once-a-month "Sacred Healing Service" were featured. At the end of this particular Sunday gathering, they had several healers available to provide a personal healing session for all who were interested. I decided to take advantage of this gift since 1) I was already present, and 2) this was something I had been thinking of doing for some time.

As Fate Would Have It

I walked out into the Garden Court after the service and there, in front of me, were about six different healers beginning their work. My eyes landed on a woman whose energy felt right to me, so I stood near and waited for my turn. I watched in admiration while she performed beautiful healing work on a woman sitting in front of her.

As my thoughts turned to my own situation, to the healing I anticipated receiving, I began looking around the room at all the wonderful healing sessions taking place. As I looked behind me, I was surprised to see the healer there was the same woman who had sat next to me in church just a few minutes ago!

With hindsight being 20/20, I can now see there was a reason why the healer I first sought out seemed to take such an extended amount of time on the person she was working with. It gave me time to turn around and see who God had really intended me to be, the person who would help facilitate my healing that day. God is always at work, and miracles happen all the time when we allow them room to do so.

The session I experienced with this woman, the very same one that had radiated such positive energy during the service, was nothing short of amazing. After asking some initial questions about what I wanted this healing to focus on, she immediately expressed that I had a lot of negative energy stored in my throat area that needed releasing. She suggested that the way to release this was to "pour love into the area," tell myself, "I don't need to store any of this in my body any longer," and then consciously release it.

With that said, she asked me to take a couple of deep cleansing breaths, close my eyes, and let the chair support me. In every sense, I could feel the release of this negative energy. It felt so freeing. The dark, bad feelings were gone. What I can tell you is that this healing session was certainly a success, and a resounding one if we were to listen to my body's reaction in the moment!

The universe had decided to put us together, and I was grateful for that incredible orchestration.

In talking with this healer afterwards, I told her that the diagnosis I had been living with was an autoimmune dis-ease that left my own body to attack itself. I shared that I could see a very real correlation between my inner and outer world, and knew that I needed to follow her advice to release the feelings stored up within me, emotions that were attacking my body. What a phenomenal day to remember on my road to wellness!

As stated earlier, the most important thing in choosing any course of treatment and/or procedure is that it fully resonates with *you*. While I do **not** advise one course of treatment over another, I would be remiss to not share what I have learned during my own personal journey towards health and well-being. What you need to do is choose what direction is best for you and see it through, just as I did for myself.

My path led me to opt-out of the only Western drug that was available for my diagnosis. I took this path after much soul searching and with open eyes and understanding of the risks I was exposing myself to by not being on the medication. That was a personal choice, and one that I had to make for myself. You are your own highest authority and the one who must choose for yourself. After doing thorough research and soul-searching, go within to ask your Higher Self, "What is right for me?"

The Best of Both Worlds

I firmly believe in using the best of Western medicine, along with considering whichever complementary and alternative options resonate with you. When all is said and done, there is simply no one route that I recommend over another. I am just, openly and honestly, sharing my experiences, which include many of the things that others thought were right for me.

Even though I put so much faith and belief in the medical community, I was confronted with a body screaming from the inside out that I could not live like this anymore. When you arrive in a similar situation, you will have to ask yourself the same question: "What is right for me?" Whatever route you take, do it because you love yourself. A great affirmation to go along with your chosen treatments is, "Every treatment I take improves my health!" while picturing yourself becoming healthier because of the power of your overwhelming belief. Let your light shine!

While some medications may change, there is one part of my daily life which will remain a constant - "OCEANS OF WELLNESS° - A Fountain of Youth." This is a permanent, 7-step system that assists both me and so many I have had the privilege to work with to live a life of excellence!

What I know for sure is that love will always be the #1 prescription for me and by me. Part of that love is intertwined with the act of forgiveness. Can you now see how both love and forgiveness are really one and the same and how essential they are to our overall health and well-being?

Forgiveness is the Gift We Give Ourselves

Even though I know that forgiveness is a powerful aspect of self-care, I still wanted to devote an entire wave to it because it has the power to change lives. While forgiveness can be challenging for most of us, it is the gift that keeps giving.

I first understood the true concept of forgiveness when introduced to the book, *A Course in Miracles*, which suggests that forgiveness is a necessity. And, by that, I am referring to both forgiveness of others as well as self-forgiveness.

Louise Hay, founder of the well-known publishing company, *Hay House*, has been one of my mentors for many years. Regarding her inspiring thoughts on forgiveness, she says that it is, "The gift we can give ourselves." To me personally, this way of thinking is nothing short of extraordinary.

Louise also states, "When we blame another, we give our power away because we are placing the responsibility for our feelings on someone else. People in our lives may behave in ways that trigger uncomfortable responses in us. However, they didn't get into our minds and create the buttons that have been pushed. Taking responsibility for our own feelings and reactions is mastering our ability to respond."

Choosing Our Reactions

In her words, "We learn to consciously choose rather than simply react." She continues, "We can't talk about resentment, without also talking about forgiveness. Forgiving someone doesn't mean that we condone their behavior."

The act of forgiveness takes place in our own mind. It has nothing to do with the other person, despite what our negative emotions might be telling us. The reality of true forgiveness lies in setting ourselves free from holding on to the pain. It is an act of releasing ourselves from that negative energy and allowing an influx of love. While negative energy accumulates and is harmful to our bodies and our health, the positive energy of love covers us with healing medicine.

In the fabulous book, *Defy Gravity: Healing Beyond the Bounds of Reason*, Caroline Myss says, "Healing comes from gathering wisdom from past actions and letting go of the pain that the education cost you." The extreme value of the forgiveness process is endless!

Shell 1: The Power of Forgiveness

We must develop and maintain the capacity to forgive. He who is devoid of the power to forgive is devoid of the power to love. There is some good in the worst of us and some evil in the best of us. When we discover this, we are less prone to hate our enemies.

– Martin Luther King, Jr.

A big realization in my life came while reading an article in Louise Hay's newsletter. She explained, "Forgiveness doesn't mean allowing the painful behaviors or actions of another to continue in your life. Sometimes, forgiveness means letting go. You forgive them and release them. Taking a stand and setting healthy boundaries are often the most loving things you can do, not only for yourself, but for the other person as well."

Why should I forgive someone who wronged me?

That's simple - you do it for you! The single most important reason to forgive is to allow yourself to lead a happy and healthy life. If someone wrongs you, then do whatever it takes to forgive and release the hurt, shame, and pain that came from their actions. Only then will your body be free of clinging to toxins that wreak havoc on your system.

Establishing healthy boundaries helped me find my way out of the chaos that was my marriage. I was finally able to make the necessary, yet tough, decision to change my life for the better. Not only that, but I was able to do so without feeling bad or guilty that the marriage failed. Most importantly, I learned to forgive and then release.

So many second chances had been given to my former husband, that the very idea of them lacked any sort of real meaning. It was empty and I knew it. I learned that I could only control what I did, and if I was going to survive, I needed to remove myself from the situation to protect me and my son. If you have felt the same way during the course of any of your relationships, know that you have the power to create change.

Why isn't forgiving the same as condoning their actions?

Forgiving someone from your heart should be about you coming to terms with how you feel about the situation. If something horrible happens or someone does a heinous crime, you are not going to just decide that this is perfectly fine behavior in order to forgive.

Instead, you are going to come to terms with the understanding that there is a reason for everything and good can come from life's great tragedies. You need to come from a place of grace and forgiveness and release any and all pain that you may have endured. When you do this with a spirit of honesty and sincerity, you will do great things for your health and well-being.

Sometimes getting out of a bad situation is a very serious matter in itself. Looking back, I realize I had no idea what I was dealing with, and wish that I would have enlisted the support of a professional to help me navigate those mine fields of negativity.

I have since learned the overwhelming importance of letting go of the past. Live in the present and let go of regrets. And then, once you have let them go, think about the good that came from the difficult times. These challenges were important in molding you into the fabulous person you are today! They have made you stronger than you have ever been before.

These are only a few of the gifts we receive from adverse situations. Let go of what is weighing you down, and set yourself free from the pain of the past so you can walk boldly and confidently into your new and bright future.

Shell 2: The Streets of My Mind

> **❝To forgive is to set a prisoner free and discover that the prisoner was you.❞**
>
> – Lewis B. Smedes

I love when my mentor and friend, Mary Morrissey, reminds me that, "It must be safe for others to cross the streets of my mind." What she is referring to is releasing resentment. We need to get to the point where it is safe for a particular person, one who we feel has harmed us, to enter into our thoughts and not be subjected to our harmful thinking towards them. It is a beautiful freedom when we can genuinely wish them well and let them be on their way. This is quite simply an act of self-preservation.

What do you mean my thoughts are in need of protection?

Many of our thoughts are influenced by what others say, do, or feel. And, when we are not careful, we sometimes allow the negativity, fears, uncertainties, and just plain hang-ups of others to interfere with our well-being. For example, how many times have you had sleepless nights over what someone said or did to you? Exactly. When this happens, you are—in fact—holding yourself prisoner to their influence. For this very reason, we need to protect the streets of our minds and make sure they are filled with positive and loving thoughts.

Let me ask you a question - would you put yourself in a prison cell with hardened criminals and try to live these life-enhancing principles in that environment? Or, would you like to keep your mind clear and surrounded by people and things that uplift you? They say we are the sum of the five people we spend the most time with.

With this in mind, it is imperative to our health and happiness that we choose wisely and surround ourselves with people who are not only healthy and positive themselves, but also nurture our spirit.

When we do this, just by being around those who are positive and generous in nature, we get swept up in this joyful energy and naturally begin to feel more positive and generous ourselves.

How do I protect myself without closing down?

At times, navigating the line between trusting others and protecting ourselves may feel like a slippery slope. Just know that finding your balance is very possible, and it comes down to drawing a line in the sand and standing up for yourself when necessary. Once you know your boundaries and what you will and will not tolerate, your newfound confidence will help you navigate those slopes.

What is really important is that when we have been let down, betrayed, or harmed in some way, we are able to practice forgiveness and wish the other person well. Even though it may be hard to accept in the moment, they came into our lives for a purpose. It is vital that we extend forgiveness to others as well as to ourselves. This is the true self-forgiveness work that is critically important for our health and well-being and for living a life of excellence.

Shell 3: The Shift

> *❝I must have decided wrongly because I am not at peace. But, I can choose again.❞*
>
> – A Course in Miracles

When we begin to understand the power of how we perceive others' actions, we give ourselves the ability to decide how it affects us. We begin to see all of the options available when we learn to look with soft eyes. While this does not mean that we are going to allow someone to do things to us that are inappropriate, it does help us to pause and see that there has to be some level of hurt on their part to inspire this sort of behavior. I think we can all agree that a truly happy person would not behave in such negative ways, signaling that person's actions as a call for love.

I know this desperation to be true, especially in regards to my former husband. In looking back, all of his misbehavior was really one big call for love after another. Clearly these were the calls of someone who was hurting inside.

How does a call for love result in hurting others?

There are various degrees of hurt and anger, but these incidents of lashing out come from an inner hurt. I chose not to face it at the time, but my husband would occasionally mention his inner demons. I would think to myself, "Oh my gosh, I don't want to hear that," and pretend that I didn't hear what he said. That too has been a learning lesson that showed me the need to face things early on. Like Mary Morrissey says, "It's best to shovel while the pile is small."

You are so much better off handling things when they are still relatively small than waiting for them to spiral out of control. I did not always practice this myself, but believe me that it is a much better way to live. In my human resources position, I often told people, "You are so much better off handling something when it is small. Do not wait until it is a storm."

How do we change our perceptions and see with soft eyes?

The answer is simple - with love. True love and compassion prevail when we soften our hearts and look through eyes of acceptance. If we were to walk in their shoes, would we be any different?

It is the same thing with red flags in our lives. If we take note while the problem is still manageable, we give opportunity for the negative behavior to stop. Even if we said something unpleasant to someone and our tone was sharper than we would have preferred, we have the ability to correct it right then and there. This forward thinking cleans the slate and allows our relationships to move forward. Once we agree to this way of living, the feelings of grace are reflected back on us, leading to further happiness and a bettering of our health.

Even when I have said or done something that was out of line, if I address it then and there, my own body feels better physically. It is much easier dealing with things when they are a ripple than when they swell to become a tidal wave!

Shell 4: A Gift to Myself

66*Forgiveness is the fragrance that the violet sheds on the heel that has crushed it.*99

- Mark Twain

There is a part of my regular wellness practice that I am particularly fond of, the "OCEANS OF WELLNESS' Release Ceremony." This ceremony delivers the enormous gift of experiencing a highly emotional release and allows us to draw a line in the sand that lets us stand in a place that is refreshing and enveloped in a healthier perspective. This simple, yet very special, ceremony allows us to quite literally put toxic emotional baggage behind us and experience the magnificent release of an unpleasant or painful situation.

What if I am not comfortable doing a ceremony?

Let me ask you this, is it more comfortable living with the pain and discomfort of your challenges? I am sure you will agree that the potential rewards are likely to outweigh the consequences of keeping those toxic emotions and experiences held tightly within your body. My suggestion is to allow yourself to be uncomfortable for the sake of receiving this gift. This transformation begins with grace.

There are definitely times when you need to stand up for your health and treat yourself to the well-deserved gift of life itself. Whether it is uncomfortable or not, whether it is in your nature or not, it is imperative to your overall well-being to do so. It is not selfish; it is a time for replenishing yourself in more ways than you can even imagine.

Go ahead, and give yourself permission to be healthy in all ways; find this health in your body, mind, and soul. We are looking for a full-spectrum body of wellness, and this can only be achieved when you treat yourself well. And, in turn, you will then treat others with that same love and kindness.

Is this where I can finally draw that line in the sand?

Yes, absolutely yes! There has never been a better time for you to take a stand and to treat yourself in the best way you possibly can. No one knows how many tomorrows they will have, so make the most of each and every day. Draw your line in the sand, and only accept into your life that which is good and in complete alignment with your entire being. I am confident you will find awe-inspiring results!

Remember, holding onto resentment and grudges is allowing toxicities to live inside us. This is like drinking poison and expecting the other person to die. Your own health and well-being is on the line, and that needs to be a primary motivation. As we looked at before, our inner pharmacy needs to be pushed to release all of these toxins and toxic thoughts in order to allow beautiful, sparkling, healing chemicals to steep all of our cells in healing. For this reason, it is worth taking a deep dive into the rolling wave of grace.

Grains of Sand:

As one of your *Be Well!* practices, I am going to invite you to perform a release ceremony for yourself. Below, you will find step-by-step instructions for how to perform this exercise. I am confident that you will see the benefits of this beautiful practice as it works in your body.

This practice was birthed from a poem I was inspired to write while visiting a very special place in Concord, Massachusetts. While sitting on a log on the beautiful shores of Walden Pond, I felt an urge to release my thoughts. Thankfully, a friend had a pen and paper on hand, and what happened next for me was the Divine revealed in nature:

Walden Pond

To the Spirit of my being,

I claim the great I AM!

I have discovered my true essence

and the authenticity is the

grandest I can comprehend.

Thank you sweet Spirit for loving me so.

Thank you sweet Spirit for letting me know.

The beauty of this pond

is the beauty of us all,

surrounded in your love of all.

Thank you sweet Spirit for loving me so.

- *Kathryn Ford, May 24, 2013*

These were the words that were just bursting to come out of me. Inspired by this beautiful setting and the energy of Henry David Thoreau, the amazing OCEANS OF WELLNESS˚ - Release Ceremony was birthed! What an amazing experience to have! These words were literally coming through me in the moment, and I was freely—without question—spilling them onto the paper.

So, as my gift to you, I encourage you to in turn give yourself the gift of this beautiful ceremony. It will help to initiate the healing and release of any toxicity that may be held within your body. If you choose to do this, you will enter into the experience of what I call "grace."

Be Well! Exercise #4: Take part in your very own OCEANS OF WELLNESS˚—Release Ceremony. For this exercise, you will need the following items:

* Paper
* Pen
* A rock
* A body of water

Begin this practice by finding a quiet space where you are able to reflect and collect your thoughts. Once you feel centered, choose something you wish to release or something that no longer serves your highest good.

This may be a grudge you are holding on to, or maybe there is something holding you back, such as a lingering sense of self-doubt. This grace practice may need to be extended towards someone you feel has wronged you in some way, or, it may need to be turned inward and extended to yourself.

Once you have opened up to what you are being called to release, begin writing out your feelings on a sheet of paper. Writing activates an entirely new center of the brain, and its power should be appreciated. Take time and make sure to write all your emotions and feelings on the paper.

The Physical Release of Emotions

Once you have written down all that is calling out to you to be released, it is time to wrap and scrunch the paper around the rock you have chosen. This will be your "sacred vehicle" that will allow for the physical release of emotional blocks. What we must remember here is that our physical and emotional bodies are tightly connected. This is why the physical component of this ceremony has proven to be essential.

Now, take your rock to the ocean, sea, river, stream, lake, pond, or any other representation you have available for a body of water. If you are in an area where this is not possible, such as the desert, I recommend burning your paper and collecting the ashes.

Before releasing the written emotions wrapped around your rock, carefully cradle them in the open palms of your hands and say,

"Thank you, Sweet Spirit for loving me so. Thank you Sweet Spirit for letting me know that this release needed to happen."

Now, in whatever way resonates with you, throw or toss your rock. With the emotions wrapped around it, send it as far out into the body of water as you can. When you see it break the surface and sink out of sight, say, "Thank you, Sweet Spirit for loving me so."

Again, if you are not able to be present at a large body of water, simply burn your paper, collect the ashes, and flush them down the toilet while speaking the words outlined above.

The key here is the cleansing nature of the water as it takes our negative feelings away forever. It truly feels amazing to experience the release after this profoundly powerful ceremony. And, if you are willing, I invite you to email me at Kathryn@kathrynford.com and share your experiences with this life-changing ceremony.

WAVE SIX
JOY

We must always strive to remember that happiness is a choice. True joy comes from experiencing that feeling inside where the energies of wonder, well-being, love, and excitement coalesce. You can feel it moving around your entire being as your body's pharmacy releases healing chemicals that support your health and well-being. It is the most natural and effective medicine there is. When we are anchored in feelings of happiness and joy, we allow ourselves an opportunity to release any toxic weights that may be clinging to us. Experiencing overwhelming amounts of joy leads us to embracing a life of excellence and vibrant health!

Happiness Is a Choice

> 66 *We are truly blessed to have the power within us to create all that we desire.* 99
>
> – Kathryn Ford

By now, I am sure you can see just how important it is for each and every one of us to live a life that is not only exceptional, but is also drenched in excellence. In order to live this kind of life, we must be conscious about choosing the things that support us in this quest. Two areas we have total control over are our levels of happiness and joy.

The great news is that there is an endless supply of both happiness and joy just waiting to be had; it is your choice how much you allow into your life.

The primary reason I have made my coaching practice my life's work, is a desire to spread the infinite happiness I have found. I want you to have unbounded stores of happiness and joy in your life as well!

To understand how we can allow these healing elements to run free, let's dive into this business of joy a little deeper, shall we? We are going to take a deep dive to discover what joy entails and how we can get more of it in our lives.

Live A Life of Excellence

What do you suppose is the true definition of joy? For me, it is contained in my journal entries from my vacation in Florida.

166

That was a time in my life when I can honestly say I was completely filled to the brim with happiness and joy! Just take a look at what my journal reveals about the time I spent basking under the Florida sun.

"Welcome to paradise! The sun is beginning to rise over the island and all creatures are awakening. It appears to be another glorious day in Marco Island, Florida! The ocean is beginning to show signs of life with the first catches of the day belonging to the pelicans. New beginnings gently present themselves through the continuous lullaby of waves that played steadily throughout the night.

The orchestra of paradise is beginning to play, as I sit on the balcony and watch the day unfold in front of me. Dolphins are dancing just offshore, where they too are a beautiful sign of all that lies beneath the water. Their graceful rhythm is another reminder that all is exceptionally well. It is a new day, beginning so full with potential and the magic can be felt everywhere."

That, my friends, is the definition of what constitutes pure joy for me! You may even be able to feel the energy lifting right off these pages. This particular morning was just one of many that I experienced during a wonderful visit to Marco Island. But, in truth, this overwhelming wonder could have been anywhere on any day. Joy is about seeing and placing our attention on what brings us happiness and fulfilment in any given moment. The magical practice of allowing joy into our lives cascades into even greater pools of happiness.

This is just another example of the proven fact that we get more of what we focus on! The example I provided, soaking in the rich atmosphere of a peaceful island, is an expression of self-care and self-love. So now, I ask you to invest several minutes of your time into exploring what makes you come alive and what it means to extend love to yourself.

Contemplate and have fun with this! You will soon find yourself practicing self-care and self-love in ways you never even imagined. Not only that, but you can be an active participant in an enrichening of your own well-being and health.

Nourishing the Spirit

Enjoying The Little Things in Life

> 66*Cheerfulness is the best promoter of health and is as friendly to the mind as to the body.*99
>
> – Joseph Addison

For me, the ocean has always been a source of great healing, and its effects are deeper than I can comprehend. As mentioned, the above excerpt from my journal was written at one of my favorite places in the world, the beach on Marco Island. I invite you to take my hand as we move to the next portion of this book, where we will explore and implement these concepts on a whole new level.

Play along with me here, and let us imagine that we are having a conversation while sitting on the beach on Marco Island. I will begin by telling you just how much "I love being here after a three-year absence…"

Hand in Hand

In looking back and connecting the dots, I now see that the past three years were a rebirthing process for me. Today, my life looks nothing like it did before the process began. The last time I was here in March of 2009, I was in a marriage of 23 years, and I appeared to have a wonderful, normal life. Even as I was facing MS with both fear and resiliency, I was diligently following my every other day injection schedule; I was doing the best I could.

But that was just how things appeared. In truth, I was in the process of ending an emotionally abusive relationship that was undermining every aspect of my life. Three years later, I was set free and realized that I held the keys to a wonderful life. This gave me the renewed strength to face my diagnosis of NMO with courage and faith. And, best of all, I felt profoundly alive.

This process came with a pain so extreme, that at times I felt I could not possibly move through it. I did not know if I would ever be okay. But, like most births, at the end of excruciating pain lies the beauty of creation. Over time, the memories of these agonizing moments seemed to soften, letting me see them as being worth every ounce of the pain. In this process, I have found health and healing through the power of my faith.

I have come home to Marco Island to reconnect with paradise. I am one with "I Am that I Am." The sights, the sounds, the smells, and the warm sun fill the air with healing energy. I am allowing the energy of nature to heal my wounds and erase my pain. Welcome to paradise, Kathryn. Welcome home!

The island is filled with treasures, and some of my personal favorites are the many varieties of shells, sand dollars, and starfish. Beauty, peace, harmony, tranquility, and oneness are everywhere; I cannot help but feel how this compilation so perfectly nourishes the soul.

The very first morning we arrived, I felt a daybreak "shelling" outing to be fitting. During the previous night, the seas were rough and the waves crashed in with great force. Much to my delight, and from my experience as a seasoned "sheller," I knew this usually meant fantastic shells would populate the beach.

With great anticipation, my friend and I set our alarms to wake us before sunrise so we could be the first ones on the beach to uncover what the waves had washed ashore.

The next morning, the alarm went off and there was a split second of hesitation. Should we stay in bed and get some much-needed sleep to recover from our hectic day of travel? Or should we push ourselves out of bed and see what gems we may find?

This was my friend's first time shelling, and her enthusiasm made the decision. My exhaustion quickly turned to excitement for the adventure that was in store. We put on our aqua socks, grabbed our flashlights, and made our way to the beach. There was a treasure chest of shells sparkling in the light of our flashlights; so many had washed up in piles on the beach that we found ourselves feeling as if we had hit the jackpot.

Drawing on my previous shelling experience, where rough waters would deliver troves of treasures from the sea, I now see a perfect reflection in the pond of my life. The rough waters of my life have crashed and roared, but when the morning breaks, gifts are revealed.

I was so grateful that my friend was able to experience this amazing moment. The real beauty of shelling is seeing how each shell is unique and delicate, yet so strong. Strong enough to withstand the roughest of seas. Much like those shells, we are strong enough to withstand any challenges that come our way. I truly believe if we remember that we are made in God's likeness and rely on our Higher Self, we can and will withstand anything. We have the power to accomplish every one of our dreams. My journey is living proof. As some would say, "If I can do it, anyone can!"

There is an even deeper meaning hidden in the treasures of the sea. In addition to the many varieties of shells that find their way to shore, a sand dollar may wash up from time to time. This happens despite the overwhelming odds stacked against it.

Delicate, yet so strong, this little treasure holds a lovely surprise inside. Within the shell, you can find five "Doves of Peace," remnants of a sand dollar's five teeth. The symbolism is astounding. It is my belief that, sometimes, we just need to let go of whatever it is we are holding on to. This process of release allows us to find the peace we so desperately long for.

As a young child, I was fascinated by the life of Helen Keller. I remember learning about her and being so in awe of her outlook on life; this positivity came despite her severely challenged body. She was a superstar to me then, and still is today! Just as Helen Keller viewed her own blindness and deafness as an essential component to her calling in life, I view my NMO diagnosis as a catalyst for me to realize and live out my own calling.

Don't Wait for Permission to Live

I would not be the person I am today if not for my dis-ease. That diagnosis has been the most significant element in my journey thus far. It has cultivated the essence of my true spirit and has allowed me to experience the Divine as a vessel of grace and optimism within my own life.

170

So please, don't wait for permission to live your life! The biggest regrets people have are for the things they *didn't* do.

As Harriet Beecher Stowe said, "The bitterest tears shed over graves are for words left unsaid and deeds left undone."

As stated earlier, our power to create a life of excellence is present in this very moment. Make sure you give yourself permission to make the most out of each and every day. Let go of the worrying, the regrets, and the fears that can be so overwhelming in the midst of a challenge. Soak in what the present moment offers, no matter what setbacks you may be facing, and be sure to move gracefully through any lingering remnants of grief or shock.

Again, it is normal and important to give our feelings their fair time, but then we must push any negative energy out. When we allow ourselves to spend time with our feelings, we are then able to move out of the darkness. By allowing ourselves to see what is really going on inside, we are led to transformation and healing. It is only after this process that we are finally ready to find the solutions that will propel us forward.

The Gift of Spirituality

Prior to receiving the NMO diagnosis, whenever a health setback occurred, I felt as if God had somehow abandoned me. It wasn't until my misdiagnosis came about that I was able to find a renewed sense of peace. This is one of many gifts my spiritual practices have bestowed upon me on my journey - a feeling of never being alone.

I was finally able to digest this reality on a deeper level after reading a poem entitled *Foot Prints* (more on this beautiful poem later). It was after, when I finally felt the comforting warmth of His arms around me, that I was ready to stop blaming God for not being there for me during the difficult times.

Over the years, studies have been done on the power of prayer. The results that have come back are so extraordinary that they can't always be explained. However, it has been found that people who are ill and have others praying for them—even though they might not be aware of this prayer—tend to have better outcomes than those who are not the recipients of the magnificent energy of prayer.

No matter how difficult it may be to see in the moment, God's impact runs far and wide. Rest easy knowing that there is a bigger picture and you are an amazing part of it.

Happy People Make Other People Happy

66 Those who bring sunshine to the lives of others cannot keep it from themselves. 99

– James Barrie

First and foremost, we must deeply love ourselves. Second, we must know that happiness is a choice. We have the power to create the life we want. Creating a life where you feel good—both physically and emotionally—is often brought about by making other people happy. And, the best way to make other people happy is to be happy yourself! For as long as I can remember, my motto has been, "Happy people help make others happy."

Happiness is a magical energy that continues to circulate as long as we allow it into our lives. Remove the focus from what has gone wrong and re-center on all that is going right! It is your primary job to maximize your own happiness. Make this shift in your life today, and prepare for the miracles to come.

While attending a graduation party for the daughter of a friend, one of the other guests asked me, "What is the most important key to living both a life of excellence and to thriving." My answer - "I believe it includes two important aspects, which are 'love' and 'joy,' and that both of these are within our control."

One way I took control of my life was by becoming a certified *Life Mastery Consultant*, and also a *Dream Builder Coach*, through Mary Morrissey's *Life Mastery Institute*. Why I chose this certification was twofold. First, it is a spiritual-based program with principles that align perfectly with my life and experiences. Second, I feel strongly that even though we may have health challenges, this does not mean we should abandon our dreams. This rings true even in the face of a devastating diagnosis.

Going after my dreams has brought me infinite happiness. Every single day, I give thanks for the opportunity to be able to do what I do - give people the necessary tools to find their own happiness. Found through my own experiences of over 27 years with a dis-ease, these tools allow anyone to make the rest of their life be the best of their life. The gift of a life filled with full-spectrum wealth is waiting to be unwrapped.

Make the World Your Playground

Living a life of choosing happiness fills your world with pure joy. To live this way is to make the world your playground; and, wouldn't you believe, that this allows for more and more love and joy to blossom! There are very few things more incredible than watching your life transform with one quantum leap after another.

I firmly believe that allowing ourselves to dream big, creating our own "Personal Passion Prescription" (which is a practice taught exclusively in my "OCEANS OF WELLNESS˚ - A Fountain of Youth" coaching program), and putting all these wellness techniques into practice each and every day, leads to the realization of our favorite dreams.

Manifested dreams, simply and profoundly, allow us to live a life of excellence. They open a path for us to thrive. And so, part of living a life of excellence and making the world my playground was to expand my own horizons. I wanted to get closer to the ocean that has always made me feel so alive. When I turned fifty years old, my dream was to move from Minnesota to California. I wasn't sure how I was going to make this happen, but I knew it was in my stars.

Now, as part of my own discovery process, I have learned that balance, the kind that is present in every part of my life, is vitally important. It was this discovery that led me to see the power of the climate we live in.

For those that don't know, Minnesota weather swings from one extreme to the other. The summers are hot and humid, and the winters are blisteringly cold. I noticed that these swings not only had a direct effect on how much time I was able to spend outside, but they also dictated the messages my body was sending me. It was pleading with me to understand that the weather outside was not in harmony with my health.

Now, with all of that being said, I have many friends and family members who find Minnesota weather to suit them perfectly. The change of seasons and the stunning beauty of the land of 10,000 lakes resonates with them. So, I am not saying my path is the path for everyone, simply that it is necessary that your path resonates with *you*!

During my process of discovery, frequent travel to the Los Angeles area for various meetings had started to reveal to me that my body was responding very positively to the climate. Was it because I was in the "City of Angels" and next to a peaceful ocean? Or, was the connection something that my mind, body, and spirit latched onto? The second question reveals the true answer. Even though I couldn't yet put it into words, the unmistakable connection was something I could feel to my core!

It became perfectly clear to me that there were changes I needed to make in my life. So, with that self-discovery underway, I began to dream big! My dream included not just moving to California, but moving to Santa Monica. And not just Santa Monica, but right next to the world-famous Santa Monica beach.

In order to make my dream life a reality, I enlisted the support of a coach for myself! With Mary Morrissey's loving support, I was able to squeeze my four-year plan to move from Minnesota to California into just four months.

In four short months, my home was sold for nearly the asking price, a twenty-year collection of items was cleared away, and I was living at the beach with only the things that I considered to be truly meaningful to me!

Having Support to Follow Your Dreams

I am so very grateful to Mary for all of her love and support in making my dream come true so quickly. The most precious gift we have is our time, and without her support and guidance, I might still be trading mine for living in a climate that did not support my mind, body, or spirit.

This is exactly the type of quantum leap that I now have the privilege of helping my clients take in their own lives! My goal is to help them find their own excellence, whether that might come in the form of training someone to encourage their cells to regain their health; finding the love of their life; discovering work that they are passionate about; creating more wealth; or even learning how to work smarter rather than harder in order to experience more precious time.

A Work in Progress

Soak in All That Life Has to Offer

❝*To the mind that is still, the whole universe surrenders.*❞

– Lao Tzu

One June, back in Minnesota, a friend and I were in the middle of the second largest lake in the state, Mille Lacs Lake. It is so big that the water fades into the horizon, always reminding me of the ocean. With the shore at your back, the vast blue water stretches towards the sky. The puttering of the motor was barely noticeable in the background as the sunlight danced on the surface of the deep, blue water. It was one of the most gorgeous days on planet earth, and it took place in the land of 10,000 lakes, beautiful Minnesota!

Our fishing lines were cast, and our hope was to catch a fairly large walleye. As I was writing in my journal, a tiny spider crawled across the paper. I thought to myself how wonderful it was, as the feeling of being one with nature and all of God's creation spread its healing touch. I paused my writing and watched this tiny being navigate his way across the paper. Next to the vastness of the gigantic body of water we were floating on, the spider was but a beautiful, detailed speck. And yet, both the spider and the body of water came together to carry a sense of calmness and peace throughout my body. It was a raw scene of living in the present moment, enjoying the luxury of an afternoon full of peace and tranquility.

An hour later, I realized we had not met our goal of catching any fish. However, the real purpose of our adventure was to nourish the soul; that goal had already been met! So, while we may have appeared to be waiting to catch "the big one," we were never really waiting at all. Remind yourself daily to live in the moment, and watch in wonder as your days light up your life!

This is a simple yet elegant example of how we should never place nourishing our spirits on hold. There is no reason why we cannot cherish everyday moments while striving to live in the present. This is how we live in the now and how we soak in all the beauty that life has to offer.

This brings me right back to why I do what I do. I love living a full and amazing life, and believe you should have that opportunity as well. There is no one that deserves anything less! And, even in the face of serious health challenges, I have found ways to live a life of excellence. Take comfort in that; if I can find a way to let love abound and enhance every aspect of my life, the same can be true for you.

Being in the Present Moment

A favorite passage of mine reads, "Stay in the moment, the present moment. The gift of the present moment is the greatest gift of all, because in reality the present moment is all we have. The past is behind us and the future is yet to be, and all our power lies in this moment." Here in the now, we have the power to decide our future.

Let me share a quote by Margaret Runyan Castenada, which I feel sums things up so beautifully: "When you think, choose carefully. The thoughts of things you'd like to be - thoughts entertained in the minds of men, become tomorrow's objectified whims." What is emphasized in her words is the fact that the thoughts we have today will shape our tomorrow. Power resides in the present.

We have complete control over our emotional state in the present moment, and it will ultimately affect our total health and well-being. While it might not always be possible to remain in complete control of our feelings, we have the power to choose how we respond. I am frequently asked, "What are we to do when someone is pushing our buttons?" This is a great question, and whenever I find myself in a trying situation, I remind myself to "keep my power" and respond from a place where I am maintaining my peace. It is when we give up our peace that we give our power to the other person.

While some might find it a difficult truth to work with, take solace in knowing that you are entirely in charge of your reaction to anything that happens. That other person, the one that is trying to take away your peace, *does not have the power to do so unless you let them*. We cannot control what happens to us, but we certainly have control over our response to it.

Remember that we will always get more of what we focus on. Allowing for worry to take over brings us a host of negative energy. In other words, the act of worrying is counterproductive to being happy. So, eliminate worry and be happy!

Pay Attention to Where Your Attention Goes

In an Oprah interview with Deepak Chopra, he explained how all pain and pleasure is dependent on where you put your attention. The following is an excerpt from Deepak's interview: "I went to a monastery in Thailand. We took our baths in the stream, we begged for our food in the streets, I shaved my head and walked barefoot. My head monk asked how it was walking. I said it hurt without shoes. And the monk then said, 'It hurts on the foot that's down, but the one that's up feels really good - so focus on that one.'"

I had to stop and reflect when I first read this. What a terrific example for all of us to hold close. We hold the power to focus on the positives in our lives; by doing this, happiness and joy will automatically follow.

Your number one takeaway from this chapter should be to always remember that happiness is a choice. I believe no matter what is happening in our lives, we have the power within us to be happy and retreat to our own place of peace.

Allow the chaos to swirl around you as you observe from the place inside of you where peace reigns. This means that you dive within, finding yourself where the comfort of the Divine is always available. Roll with the challenges and approach them with peace and acceptance. Do not let anything rob you of your divine gift of peace.

We will all draw our last breath one day, but how many of us truly live a vibrant life of excellence? I know for me, there is a constant need in my life to place a loving emphasis on *living*. As one of my favorite authors, Henry David Thoreau, said, *"I don't want to get to the end of my life and wonder what would have happened if I really lived."*

I believe in order to really live, we must release the "what ifs" and start living a life of excellence *today*. Develop dreams and goals, and treat yourself like the precious person you are. Take one step towards well-being today and learn how to take care of your needs first. As I said before, even airlines instruct us before take-off that—in the event of an emergency—we should put our own mask on first! Then, and only then, are we fully capable of helping those around us. If you are always putting yourself last, you will not have anything left for the people that need you most.

You see, you can't give away what you do not have. This is especially important to remember for those of us with health challenges. I have found along my own path, that when I don't follow my daily self-care routine, I am in no position to do any good for anyone or anything else! So, take this advice seriously, as it is critically important.

Here's to Your Exceptional Life

To a sailor with no direction, no wind is favorable.

– Anonymous

Each of us should be crystal clear as to what it is we truly want and where it is that we want to go. Without a compass to guide our journey and set our course, we are like sailors lost at sea.

With clear and steady guidance, we will be well-equipped to achieve our desires and arrive at our intended destination. I am a living example of someone who reached out for help. In finding my personal coach, I ended up charting a new course. With a clear map in hand, I was ready to navigate the seas of uncertainly and set sail for new lands.

Know Where You Are Going and Why

My coaching practice offers me the opportunity to be there for the amazing people I work with, and at the same time to truly live for me! Not only do I love helping others—people that might be in the midst of similar challenges to the ones I faced—to thrive, but my practice gives me the opportunity to create a life I love living. By living a life of excellence in the presence of a health challenge, I am an example for others that this level of success is not only possible, but there is a path that we can take to get there.

I have now come to realize that the dis-ease wasn't killing me, it was pushing me to live! The diagnosis of MS as a young adult, and subsequently the discovery of NMO 22 years later, did not happen *to* me. I now choose to see it as happening *for* me!

I love this excerpt from Abraham-Hicks publications:

"Your happiness is the most significant contribution that you could make. In your reaching for happiness, you are opening a vortex, which makes you an avenue for the well-being to flow through you. And anything that is your object of attention under those conditions, benefits by the infusion of your well-being."

Always remember that you can choose to make happiness the object of your attention! Your happiness promotes well-being, which encourages even more happiness! It is one of the laws of the universe!

When I moved to California, I chose to make living a life of excellence and full-spectrum wealth my focus. As I placed my attention on this horizon, my whole world began to take form around it. And, just like that, it became my reality! So many miracles occurred for me to start living the life of my dreams, but that is exactly what happens when our thoughts begin to move molecules. The 7-step system of "OCEANS OF WELLNESS˙ - A Fountain of Youth" is just one of the joyful miracles changing lives every day, all around the world!

Shell 1: The Energy of Wonder

> ❝I, not events, have the power to make me happy or unhappy today. I can choose which it shall be. Yesterday is dead—tomorrow hasn't arrived yet. I have just one day, today, and I am going to be happy in it.❞
>
> – Groucho Marx

Joy abound when the energy of wonder, well-being, love, and excitement are all flowing. When we are connected to joy, we are able to tap in to the powerful vibration of infinite possibility. It becomes easier to release any toxic blocks that we may be carrying.

180

For me, oceans are magical. They provide an instant sense of wonder and joy. This overwhelming joy allows the toxins that stem from stress and worry to dissipate.

How do I learn to enjoy the journey?

You can take any opportunity and turn it into a joyful experience. That being said, it takes practice to properly set your programming. The goal is to always be on the lookout for joyous experiences ready to flow into your life. Immerse yourself in the opportunities that present themselves, be open to joy, and remember that being "present in the moment" allows joy to rapidly expand!

One thing I personally do to increase my joy quotient, is to take in the beauty and detail of objects that I am drawn to. For me, the intricacies of nature fill me up. It may be a bird, a dolphin, or a small flower by the wayside. What fills your spirit?

When we examine the properties of the ocean, it allows us a window into our wellness and happiness. The sense of possibility while staring out at the horizon spans comprehension. The good news—for those that don't have access to a large body of water (or any place that gives them this feeling)—is that we can bring ourselves to the special places in our mind anytime we wish.

So, what should I do if I live in a "less than desirable" location?

First, remember the immense power of choice that you have. You are in control of your own happiness. If you live in a location that isn't nourishing your soul, you have two choices to better your situation.

Either pick up and move like I did, or turn your current situation into one that is more in tune with the life you want to be living. Start with envisioning the things that you love. Step into the realm of possibility and imagine a wonderful life and location that causes you to light up with joy each and every day.

Start to infuse some of those aspects into your everyday life. It may be as simple as bringing fresh-cut flowers or live plants into your living space. It could be changing up the blankets, comforter, or sheets that line your bed, so you can sleep every night on something you love. Or, one thing might lead to another, and you might just magically find yourself walking the shores of the Pacific!

I believe we all have a choice for how our lives turn out. The gift of deciding our own reality is up to each of us, and we can live a life of excellence regardless of our personal challenges. So, raise your glass and let out a resounding "Cheers!" to designing a healthy and fabulous life that starts today!

Shell 2: Journey to Excellence

> ❝Take a deep dive into your own inner wisdom and mastery to find a life filled with excellence.❞
>
> – Kathryn Ford

Joy, if cultivated properly, can become part of your lifestyle. It is a divine part of our journey to a life of excellence and vibrant health. I wholeheartedly believe we are meant to experience as much joy as possible. That life, the one filled with staggering waves of joy, starts today!

Open yourself to the beauty of allowing more and more joy to flow into your life. When we are free-flowing and open, we begin to look for moments that can contribute to our joy throughout the day. We begin to naturally seize opportunities to fill our lives with wonder.

What will this journey look like?

That is entirely up to you. You can take each moment in stride and have a great attitude no matter what comes your way, or you can choose to immerse yourself in the pain and anguish of life's challenges. It is up to you to choose one that makes you happy and brings you joy. It really is as simple as that!

During our eulogies, we will be remembered for who we were. It won't be about what we did for our company's market share or the things we purchased. It will be about who we were as a person, and the hearts, minds, and lives we touched.

182

Learn to appreciate all of the little things. Stand in awe and wonder for the rich and loving relationships you have cultivated. Be patient with your progress and always be kind to yourself as you learn. "Do your best, and let the good Lord do the rest."

How long will my road to wellness take?

The road to wellness is a journey that spans your entire life. There is always more to learn and more growth to be had. With that being said, I firmly believe that you can have immediate and profound results that start when you take the very first step.

Shell 3: Embrace The Lifestyle

> 66*Pearls don't just lie along the seashore.*
> *If you want one, you must dive for it.*99
>
> – Chinese Proverb

When joy becomes second nature, the health benefits can be miraculous. My wellness prescription for you is to set an intention every morning to stop and be grateful for the magnificent moments of joy that come your way. That is a lifestyle worth embracing!

I would love to see your life blossom, and for peace, happiness, and joy to flourish. Take one step after another, and stay the course.

Are there stepping stones to guide my way?

There most certainly are! While we have looked at a number of them that line the way, there are more stones that you will find on your own. You will undoubtedly uncover many of them once your journey is underway. Always remain open, and be on the lookout for new methods and techniques that resonate with your spirit.

Each of us is unique, and our paths will vary in a thousand different ways. I hope that you can learn from my personal road to wellness, and then turn within to be guided towards the practices that work best for you. And, as always, know that you deserve the best that life has to offer.

What practices are universal?

We will dive into this more in the next—and final—chapter, but for now, the following practices have shown themselves to have immense power: eat healthy, surround yourself with positivity, and always do what you can to see the best in any given situation. These three things will do wonders in jump-starting your personal wellness routine!

All in all, this wellness practice is driven by *you*. You are the one who needs to step on the gas pedal and get your vehicle moving in the direction of health. I have complete faith in you!

Shell 4: Your Spirit Loves Fun

> *“Joy sounds like a simple word, but its depth and complexity will cause you to sit back in awe.”*
>
> – Kathryn Ford

When it comes to joy and happiness, we must realize that they are both inside jobs. What feels like joy to one person may not resonate as strongly with another; this is what makes the self-discovery process vital.

When you are stretching yourself to experience more joy, there is one practice that encourages you to find what works *for you*—lean into it. Try new things and ask for your own awareness to expand. Finding your joy will differ to others finding their own. Take the time to uncover what makes you delight in the sparkling qualities of pure joy!

It is not always easy to be consciously aware of, but we should always remember that we are spiritual beings having a human experience. And here's something you will want to know about our inner Spirit—it *loves* fun! Joy sounds like a simple word, but its depth and complexity will cause you to sit back in awe.

Joy is the experience of delight, excitement, jubilation, and bliss; it is all of these feelings turned inward and leads to well-being, love, and excitement rising to the surface. It is when we cannot wait to live another day. It is a child on Christmas morning, looking at all the presents nestled under the tree. It is the new mother holding her child in her arms for the first time. Joy is contagious and comprehensive. These incredible feelings of wonder and happiness cause our spirits to thrive.

So, joy lets me have my cake and eat it too?

Yes, it does! We live in an abundant universe that has room for so much growth and opportunity. Take full advantage of the opportunities that come your way.

Again, our spirit loves to have fun. When it is lighting up like the 4th of July, the body's own pharmacy releases many healing chemicals that support your overall health and well-being. It is the most natural and effective medicine in the world.

Grains of Sand:

Hopefully, after reading this chapter, you have arrived at the understanding that happiness is a choice. It is one that can be made at any moment and at any time. It does not rely on the opinions of others; the level of happiness you experience in life is completely up to you! You have the power to decide your future.

The key to living a life of excellence is to create situations and experiences that bring you more joy. I invite you to seriously think about that statement, and to write down the things that make you happy and bring the most joy into your life. This is a great place to begin your journey towards fulfillment in all that you do. Go for it!

WAVE SEVEN
OCEANS OF WELLNESS®

The ocean saved me. It rescued me quietly, with the rhythm of each wave bringing me back to life. Whenever you need to reconnect with who you are, consider a barefoot walk along the beach. Allow the waves to cover your feet, healing your body down to the cellular level. There's a reason that people have sought out the power of the sea from the very beginning of history. The ocean has the power to heal, to wash away the difficulties in your life, and to replace them with something new. OCEANS OF WELLNESS® - A Fountain Of Youth, is an ocean lifestyle for your inner world!

Daily Prescriptions

In This Chapter

* The best practices for vibrant health
* Blueprints for living a life of excellence

> *It's not enough to have lived. We should be determined to live for something. May I suggest that it be creating joy for others, sharing what we have for the betterment of person-kind, bringing hope to the lost and love to the lonely.*
>
> – Leo Buscaglia

Like the ebb and flow of distant waves, I have always felt the ocean calling me. Whenever I need to reconnect with who I am, I try to visit my beloved ocean. It has been a pivotal part of my life and my journey, and the impact has caused me to build my entire life and coaching practice around the stretching sea.

Power Within the Waves

My "Top 21 Be Well!" Practices

> *Allow the waves of blessings in your life to wash over, cleanse, and renew you.*
>
> – Kathryn Ford

In the following pages, I have compiled a list of my top 21 practices, ones that have literally saved my life. Each and every day, I make it a mission to draw upon as many of these as possible. See which ones feel right, and then incorporate them into your own life. The moment you put the first one into action, you put yourself that much closer to a life of excellence.

There is no particular order to this list, and no one practice is more important than another. Start by working your way through them all, and then add any new discoveries of your own. By stocking your own "wellness tool box," you create a life that is filled to the brim with potential. Then, it is up to you to live out an amazing life as the magnificent person you are!

1) Laughter

The Great Mood Changer

> **"***At the height of laughter, the universe is flung into a kaleidoscope of new possibilities.***"**
>
> – Jean Houston

"Laughter is the best medicine." There is a reason that we all know this phrase; it holds so much truth. Laughter truly is the best medicine, one that is worth its weight in gold. Genuine laughter branches out to include smiling, and smiling is one of the most powerful actions we have in our personal inventory. When we smile, our chemical composition changes, providing a variety of benefits that are favorable to our health.

The next time you find yourself in a bad mood, take a deep breath. As you breathe out, set a smile on your face, and wait for your mood to lighten. When it does, soak in the feeling of goodness as it washes over you.

Throughout the years, I have come across so many people with health challenges that have made it a point to add laughter into their healthcare routine. Through shielding themselves from negativity and placing their focus on joy, they tell their body, "I am here for you, and you are number one."

For me, a few wonderful ways to guarantee regular laughter is to watch a great movie, see a comedian perform on TV (or better yet, in person), or simply surround myself with people who make it so easy for me to laugh and smile!

The people in your life play a very important role in the energy that you bring to each and every day. They can fill you up and contribute to your health, or they can drain you of precious energy. As we have learned, it is detrimental to our health when our energy stores are depleted. Always be sure to surround yourself with people who make you feel strong and encourage you to laugh and smile.

2)   Faith and Trust

The Great Comforter

66*Within you lies the simple silence. Be quiet and listen.*99

– Author Unknown

My own experiences have taught me that our universe is a friendly one. We are never alone, no matter what troubles come our way. Although my faith has provided a great deal of comfort and support, it hasn't always kept my fears at bay. There was a significant period, during some of my most challenging times, that I felt abandoned. I would find myself asking, "How could God allow such painful things to happen to someone who tries so hard to be a good person?" I have a suspicion that I am not alone in having had those feelings.

Well, I was wrong. The truth is that the Spirit has always been by my side, and I have been able to overcome the challenges in my life *because* it carried me through. I now understand and realize the depth of the words in the well-known poem, "Footprints in the Sand." Looking back, I can remember the "footprints" next to me during the difficult times.

Footprints in the Sand

"One night I dreamed I was walking along the beach with the Lord. Many scenes from my life flashed across the sky.

In each scene I noticed footprints in the sand. Sometimes there were two sets of footprints, other times there were one set of footprints.

This bothered me because I noticed that during the low periods of my life, when I was suffering from anguish, sorrow or defeat, I could see only one set of footprints.

So I said to the Lord, "You promised me Lord, that if I followed you, you would walk with me always. But I have noticed that during the most trying periods of my life there have only been one set of footprints in the sand. Why, when I needed you most, you have not been there for me?"

The Lord replied, "The times when you have seen only one set of footprints, is when I carried you." – Mary Stevenson

---

Here is my truth, and I hope that eventually you will see it reflected in your own life - if I had never been diagnosed with my dis-ease, I would still be living a fairly mediocre life. Instead, because of the challenges that have given me opportunity to rise to the occasion, I am striving to live my life to the fullest, fearlessly taking on each new day. I am able to do this thanks to the gifts my dis-ease has brought to light.

I no longer take things for granted, and I do everything I can to live in the moment. The NMO was trying to get my attention and tell me something; it was shouting to me, "Love yourself first, Kathryn!" And so, loving myself unconditionally has become my new way of living. This is my present, and it is my future. No matter how you might be feeling, no matter the challenges that might be causing you difficulty, you are never alone.

3) Nutrition

The Great Health Enhancer

❝ *Let food be thy medicine and medicine be thy food.* **❞**

– Hippocrates

Eliminating the toxins that enter our body through unhealthy or pesticide-heavy food can compound pre-existing conditions, and it can also create new ones. Having the knowledge to eat foods that your body craves can lead to a level of health you never considered possible. Often, I focus on the gut, as much of our immune system runs itself from there. Early on, one of my neurologists shared with me that we are constantly putting chemicals into our bodies by way of what we eat. From that point on, I knew that I needed to make healthy eating a priority in my life, deciding which chemicals were acceptable for my body, and which were not.

The *Macrobiotic Community Cookbook,* written by Andrea Bliss-Lerman, eloquently makes the following point: "The foods that people eat become part of them, and creating a total balance in each meal can be a practical, positive step toward creating a balance in all aspects of life. Health and happiness go hand in hand - as individuals become healthier within themselves, they are able to touch the lives of others in a way that sparks an interest in physical, mental, and spiritual health. They can also encourage others to seek a more peaceful way of life."

We eat with our eyes first, and this gives you every reason to make your meals beautiful to look at. Couple that with a warm and loving setting, and you will be doing yourself a world of good. No matter where you live, I encourage you to seek out a special place where you can comfortably enjoy eating outside. Communing with nature while you eat can bring about powerful levels of joy and gratitude. Complementing the healthy foods you take into your body with gratitude and wonder is a surefire way to take your nutrition to the next level.

Find an environment that resonates with you, whether it is alone in nature or surrounded by friends and family, and choose healthy foods. Your body will be *so grateful* for it!

4) Adequate Sleep

The Great Rejuvenator

6 6*Sleep is the golden chain that ties health and our bodies together.* 9 9

– Thomas Dekker

Optimal sleep is both restorative and rejuvenating, and is essential to one's overall health and well-being. A cool, calm, tranquil atmosphere sets the tone for optimal sleep. Firmly sticking to a sleep and wake schedule has been proven to lead to better health and an increased ability to start the next day in a well-rested and ready manner.

Finding what promotes restful and rejuvenating sleep for you may take some experimenting; everyone responds differently to different practices! One universal truth I have found is that the final moments of your day should be positive. Introducing negative thoughts before bedtime can manifest themselves in the quality of our sleep.

A more constructive approach, and one I practice, was presented in a seminar given by Dr. Wayne Dyer. In his book, *Wishes Fulfilled,* he speaks about a crucial time window—the last five minutes before we drift off to sleep. He shared how Neville Goddard (an influential metaphysics teacher and new thought author) reasons, "Whatever you have in consciousness as you go to sleep is the measure of your expression in the waking two-thirds of your life on earth."

Dr. Wayne Dyer taught his audience to use a technique that had brought about amazing results for those that tried it. He suggested the following, "Create a reminder like a prayer or mantra to place by your bed. Write these words, 'I am going to use these moments to review what I intend to manifest into my life,' and read them right before falling asleep." It is simple and effective, a truly wonderful combination!

I encourage you to try this technique, and to bring all the desires that would bring you joy to the surface. It is very little investment for a great reward.

5) Feng Shui

The Great Flow Enhancer

> ❝*In its highest and purest form, good Feng Shui signifies perfect alignment between inner and outer worlds.*❞
>
> – Lada Ray

Your environment is an extension of your physical being, and your surroundings matter. Enjoy the world around you by taking it in with all of your senses. It is important to live, laugh, and love your environment. Vibrant surroundings will most definitely contribute to your health in a positive way.

The art of Feng Shui, which deals with creating an environment full of balance, is an ancient practice with a history of proven results. One hearty definition of Feng Shui is, "An ancient art and science developed over 3,000 years ago in China, incorporating a complex body of knowledge that reveals how to balance the energies of any given space to assure the health and good fortune for people inhabiting it."

One of the basic principles of Feng Shui is that your space reflects your life. This is a fun area of study that can teach us how to implement small changes in our homes. A little at a time adds up, and before long, we will find ourselves entering our homes and feeling a surge of positive energy.

Check out a few books from your local library or research Feng Shui online, and implement the ideas that feel right for you. I highly recommend Carole Hyder's program, "The Wind and Water School of Feng Shui." I once had the privilege of hearing Carole speak, and have enjoyed implementing her concepts into my own home. She makes the concepts easy to understand, and gives practical approaches that you can get started on right away. Try to have some fun with Feng Shui, and make your home a place you can't wait to see again.

6) Managing Stress

The Great Releaser

> **Breathe through it and release everything that does not serve you.**
>
> – Unknown

Everyone has stress; it's a universal part of the human experience. That does not mean that everyone deals with it the same way. Chronic stress is a significant health hazard, and we must learn to *mitigate* it. Mitigation, which means to lessen or alleviate, keeps us reminded that there will always be stress vying for our attention. However, with the right mentality and tools, we don't have to allow it to take over.

For the sake of your physical and mental health, it is *imperative* to find ways to manage your stress. Effective practices vary by person, so taking the time and effort to find what works for *you* is a necessity. By finding the necessary tools and practices, our entire world becomes brighter.

One very effective way to manage your stress is through quiet time and meditation. There is a reason why hundreds of millions of people rave about the power of meditation. Put simply, it works.

While each and every one of these practices can help to eliminate stress, understanding their importance for your health and happiness reflects back an eternal truth—you deserve a beautiful life that is free from the toxic weight of worry. Stress will come your way, that is unavoidable, but you don't have to let it determine your future.

7) Meditation

The Great Equalizer

66 *True silence is the rest of the mind; it is to the spirit what sleep is to the body, nourishment and refreshment.* 99

– William Penn

Enjoy the holiness of your highest thoughts, and take the time to visualize them as they soothe your soul. Meditation quiets the mind. I truly believe that mind-body well-being starts here.

Meditation brings us to the still, deep place within ourselves where we can access inner calm, peace, and awareness. It gives us an opportunity to manage our fears. A healthy practice teaches us to let the winds of life swirl around us while we remain at peace in the eye of the storm. After just two months of daily meditation, this ancient practice can physically increase your brain's gray matter!

Early on, I started practicing deep breathing as a simple form of meditation. Benefits include lower blood pressure and heart rate, improved digestion, better sleep, and lower stress levels in the body. This was a very easy-to-access form of meditation that could be done anywhere at any time.

When first starting to meditate, a simple way to immerse yourself is to use a form of "guided" meditation. As a recording talks you through how you should be thinking and how to align your focus, you will learn to let yourself be comfortable with silence and an increasing familiarity with your body and thoughts.

The key to success is finding a type of meditation that resonates with you. From deep breathing to prayer, there are many different kinds of meditation. Keep trying different ones until you find the right fit for your lifestyle.

8)   Take A Deep Breath

The Great Restorer

> 66*I took a deep breath and listened to the old bray of my heart: I am, I am, I am.*99
>
> – Sylvia Plath

Dr. Oz, who many of you are likely aware of, says, "Take ten deep breaths in the morning, and another ten in the evening. Lie on your back. Put one hand on your stomach and one hand on your chest. As you inhale, push your stomach way out to the count of five. After five seconds, a comfortable breath should be held, and then slowly exhale—again, really pushing your stomach down till your belly button hits your spine."

He adds, "Making this a regular habit has three great health benefits. It makes your lungs and blood vessels function better, it helps with stress relief, and also helps with the drainage of your lymphatic system—which is the system that removes toxins from your body."

This practice also fulfills the important role of getting much-needed oxygen to all of our organs. If it sounds simple, that's because it is! So many wonderful benefits are available for us to take hold of. Sometimes, they just come in the form of something as easy as taking deep breaths!

9) Meteditative Breathing

The Great Calming Force

> 66*Another world is not only possible; she is on her way.*
> *On a quiet day, I can hear her breathing.*99
>
> – Arundhati Roy

Now we get to combine the last two tools for another easy technique for total wellness. The beauty of this meditative breathing exercise is that it has the power to reset your nervous system, lower your heart rate, and decrease your blood pressure.

This meditative breathing, technically speaking, resets our nervous system to our *parasympathetic nervous system*, which is the calming side of our nervous system, and controls our entire body. Take a deep breath in through your nose, breathing in love to the count of three. Then, hold it for another count of three and exhale through your mouth all of your cares and concerns for the count of six. Do this once, twice, and then a third time.

I highly recommend that you begin by finding a supportive chair and allowing yourself to be completely comfortable. Plant your feet on the ground and place your hands gently in your lap. Now, if you are in a safe place to do so, close your eyes. By closing our eyes, we are able to open our hearts further.

Take a moment to place your attention on your heart and focus on it, opening it just a little more, and then a little more again.

Breath in love (1, 2, 3) and hold it (1, 2, 3). Now, exhale all your cares and concerns through your mouth (1, 2, 3, 4, 5, 6).

Do this three times, each time letting love wash over you. Take a moment to enjoy the peaceful, relaxed feeling you just created for every cell in your body. As I have said before, a practice like this allows our cells to be bathed in beautiful chemicals; the prescriptions that come from the inner pharmacy have no side effects, so feel free to use them as often as you would like!

10) Beautiful Music

The Great Inspirer

> 66*Music's the medicine of the mind.*99
>
> – John A Logan

In addition to falling asleep to beautiful music, I also use it as a tool to enhance my afternoon meditation. Every single piece of music vibrates with energy. Our bodies resonate with music in this way. The vibration that happens within us is how our own being responds to the particular vibrations of specific types of music.

When we choose to listen to music that feels good, our body responds, and the effects reach all the way down to our cells. The immune system loves this, and changes occur in the presence of these magical tones. Listen to some wonderful, elegant, sweeping music to see how your body responds. Allow yourself to be caught up, and consider how you feel in the presence of these vibrations.

A word of caution: Just as music has the ability to uplift and inspire new heights of health and well-being, it can also tear down and diminish the life-force within your body. This toxicity can wear on those who constantly listen to dark, depressing, and chaotic music. Many people fail to understand how detrimental their choice in music is to their health and well-being. Be sure that the music you allow into your life carries you to places of wonder and excellence!

11) Your Sacred Sanctuary

The Great Balancer

> 66*There is a reverence for the simple, quiet pleasures of living well and beautifully at home. Home is where we return for fulfillment and wholeness.*99
>
> – Alexandra Stoddard

The home is a sanctuary for the soul. Over the years, I have found that my physical environment plays an enormous role in my total well-being. When I write, I light a candle and place it on my desk. Next to my computer is a bowl of shells from Marco Island. On the walls, I have a collage of butterflies and personal photographs. My home is filled with windows to allow both light and the beauty of nature to stream in.

Envelop yourself with surroundings that make you feel good. Curate and display treasures that emit positive feelings and energy. Make sure to allow natural light into your surroundings, as it can be a powerful boost to your energy levels. Coupled with the fact that nature is a magnificent way to connect with the Spirit, make it a habit to spend time enjoying the outdoors as often as you can.

This can be challenging if you live in the city or do not have direct access to the country. But, this just gives your creativity all the more room to shine. Find yourself a bit of green space and commit to visiting it on a regular basis. If you live in the city, a local park would be perfect.

Integrating nature into your home can be an excellent way to bridge the divide between indoors and outdoors. Fresh flowers or sprigs of lavender can sing to the senses, and are great ways to dispel any negative energy that might be hovering over you. Practice what makes you happy, and don't be afraid to bring a little bit of living beauty into your home.

12) Therapeutic Massage

The Great Relaxer

66 *The root of all health is in the brain. The trunk of it is in emotion. The branches and leaves are the body. And, the flower of health blooms, when all parts work together.* 99

– Kurdish Folk Wisdom

Massage, as a healing tool, has been around for thousands of years. However, we now have scientific proof of the benefits—ones that range from relaxation and stress relief all the way to treating chronic illness and injuries. Not only are there specific physiological and psychological changes that come about from massage, but increased benefits are found when massage happens on a regular basis. Need I say more?

Some experts estimate that up to 90% of illness is somehow related to stress. Massage and other types of body work can directly lower stress levels, helping our bodies remember what it means to relax.

If that wasn't enough to get you onboard, massage also increases circulation, stimulates the flow of the lymphatic system, relaxes muscles, and reduces spasms and cramping. It can also increase joint flexibility and release endorphins—the body's natural painkillers—as well as relieve migraine pain. There are even some studies which have shown massage to decrease levels of damaging cortisol.

As we looked at earlier, my personal experience with massage increased circulation to the skin areas around my injection sites. This was a bright spot in a difficult time, so my fondness for massage can't be overstated! I hope that you explore the benefits of massage and see the rewards play out in your overall health and well-being.

13) Acupuncture

The Great Holistic Stimulator

66*It is more important to know what sort of person has a disease than to know the disease a person has.*99

– Hippocrates

Acupuncture is an ancient Chinese art that has been around for more than 5,000 years. I have used acupuncture as an alternative treatment, and I am amazed by its effectiveness. It stimulates the body's ability to heal itself, and is rooted in traditional Chinese medicine, which is a holistic practice that treats the whole person - their mind, body, and spirit. The World Health Organization has identified more than 40 physical ailments that respond well to acupuncture, but I believe the list is much longer than that! If this feels like it resonates with you, I highly encourage you to try it.

While the very idea might frighten some people—after all, needles aren't always the most pleasant of sights—I encourage you to give it a try. By targeting specific areas on the body, acupuncture can jumpstart self-healing and promote healthy body functions. Give it a try and see if it works for you!

14) Aromatherapy and Scent

The Great Ambiance Creator

66*I invite you to drink in the divine nectar of aromatic love and let it penetrate you in the deepest, most profound ways. Trust that the oils are working to heal, regenerate, and teach you. The more you use them, the more they'll reveal their secrets to you.*99

– Elana Millman

Essential oils, or even scents from a candle or other diffusing method, can be very effective in promoting better health and well-being. In particular, lavender, chamomile, lemon, and vanilla are known to be exceptionally relaxing smells.

For me, lit candles are spiritual in nature, and set the mood for relaxation. I would also recommend that you think about purchasing a diffuser, which allows you to put in a few drops of your favorite essential oil, and then sit back as it lightly sends the smell around the room.

Personally, I most often use a lemon essential oil, as it is said to promote detoxification and purification. Do some experiments to discover which scents speak to you. Spread some candles throughout your home, and let their aromas bring you to a calmer, more peaceful place. Not only can this area of discovery be lots of fun, but it can also be affordable to try a variety of options.

15) Holistic Health Practitioner

The Great Alternative Remedy

> 66*I am not afraid of storms for I am learning how to sail my ship.*99
>
> – Louisa May Alcott

Many holistic health practitioners are able to prescribe remedies to help with balancing your system and alleviating painful conditions. This includes help with stress, allergies, and balancing your adrenals to regain lost energy. Finding balance in the body is a huge factor in determining the quality of our lives.

I prefer to use the recommendations of people I trust to find my wellness practitioners. If you don't know anyone who uses a holistic health practitioner in your area, you may want to start with your local healthcare clinic and see whether they have a list of chiropractors they might recommend. From there, you can ask for personal references; perhaps they even have a list of other holistic practitioners in the area.

When I was first looking for alternative doctors that resonated with me, it only took one to start. After I had heard about the first great practitioner, that connection opened up a whole new world of people who had made it their purpose in life to help those with health challenges. Even so, as integrative and complementary medicine keep growing in popularity, you may be fortunate to already know someone that has found a highly-regarded practitioner. Make sure that whoever you choose to build your wellness with is able to meet your specific needs.

16) Spiritual Prayer

The Great Restorer

66*If the only prayer you ever say in your entire life is thank you, it will be enough.*99

– Meister Eckhart

Regardless of your beliefs, connecting with a higher power is another way to reduce stress. Spiritual prayer, communicating with a higher presence in any number of ways, is an expansive practice. It is a way of communing with the entirety of the universe, and often includes being in nature and allowing one's self to connect with all of creation.

This feeling of "oneness" can be incredibly calming. As mentioned before, experts recommend spending some part of each day outside to let yourself be at peace with nature. Taking that time to relax and enjoy the world around you can be monumental for your health and well-being.

Gratitude is another form of spiritual prayer. As we saw back in Wave Two, gratitude is the open door to abundance in every area of our lives! Every time fear creeps in, focusing on the things you love transforms those negative feelings and brings about gifts that might otherwise be difficult to see.

I strongly suggest that you engage in this form of spiritual prayer by writing your thoughts down in a gratitude journal. I find that this practice returns me to my source of power and grounds me in strength, driving the fears away.

17) Move Your Body Everyday

The Great Energizer

> 66 *Take care of your body. It's the only place you have to live.* 99
>
> – Jim Rohn

I firmly believe, no matter the circumstances, everyone can exercise. Yes, you heard me right. *Everyone* can exercise! Of course, finding the appropriate exercise for your lifestyle and abilities is critical.

Exercise is imperative to health and well-being. According to Dr. Timothy Vollmer of the Rocky Mountain MS Center, "There are three separate goals of exercise: good general health, maximizing your current functioning, and protecting your brain for the future." Despite any thoughts you might have of exercise leading to exhaustion and fatigue, those beliefs couldn't be more false! Exercise actually *helps* with fatigue. It sounds counter-intuitive, I know, but it actually works. Whether walking every day, or—if that's not an option—doing exercises from a chair, moving your body in some way brings about newfound levels of energy.

Trust me when I say, your mind will thank you too. Physical activity steps up the production of certain proteins that encourage growth of neural connections in the brain, keeping it happy and healthy. In addition, the release of endorphins and other feel-good chemicals in your body are great for your overall well-being and outlook on life.

Exercise also helps decrease anxiety, relieves tension, improves sleep, and can reduce stress. It can also boost your metabolism, causing you to look and feel better!

One of my favorite forms of exercise is yoga. Not only does it double as a meditation tool, but it also provides all of the benefits listed above. I recommend taking a yoga class from an experienced instructor, so that you can correctly learn each pose. And, as always, before you begin any new exercise program, ask your doctor what level and intensity is suitable for you. Choose an exercise that you enjoy, and have fun with it!

18) Tapping

The Great Interrupter

66*I have found a new understanding of the emotional aspects of my pain through the use of tapping. It is truly miraculous.*99

– Kathryn Ford

Meridian tapping, also known as EFT, is a healing tool based on the body's subtle energy systems and meridians. By touching specific areas of the body, you are able to reduce negative emotions by signaling the brain to react with a sense of calm.

The process has been shown to dramatically reduce cortisol levels, which in turn reduces stress. It can be used for overcoming a variety of fears, as well as for effective pain relief, since tapping approaches pain from an emotional angle.

In other words, we target what might be hidden or stored as pain in the body, and use this pain as a window to see what stress, anger, or anxiety is hiding behind it. Tapping can heal the emotional conflicts that may contribute to your physical problems, ones that may have been draining your immune system, making you vulnerable to additional physical challenges.

As expert tapper Nick Ortner explains, "Tapping diminishes the 'noise' that surrounds us and increases the mental, emotional, and even physical responses we produce when faced with life challenges." I have found this to work on headaches, as well as other symptoms I experience from the NMO.

If this sounds like something you may want to explore, there are many excellent books and videos available to get you started. Not only is it easy and fun, but it works!

With tapping, you are able let go of the emotions that might be holding you back, and your body is allowed to recover and heal itself as the presence of fear is diminished. Where fear is replaced by peace, your health and well-being can flourish.

19) Cleaning House

The Great Liberator

> ❝It takes a lot of courage to release the familiar and seemingly secure, to embrace the new. But there is no real security in what is no longer meaningful. There is more security in the adventurous and exciting, for in movement there is life, and in change there is power.❞
>
> – Alan Cohen

As noted before, our environment has a huge impact on our overall well-being, which is why clearing out the clutter is extremely important. Clutter includes paper piles, broken appliances, old emails, clothes in the closet that are no longer worn, and even toxic people. The environment we live in either steals energy or fuels it. If the people and objects in your environment do not bring you energy, it is time to clean house. Make space for the new by releasing the old. Taking control of your environment reflects back on your inner self.

When facing health challenges, this area becomes critical. The more we can do to bring a sense of control, peace, and tranquility to our lives, the better off we are. When discerning whether something—or someone—is good for my health and well-being, I ask myself the following questions:

* Is it worthy of my time?
* Is it worthy of my energy?
* Does this make me feel good?
* Do I feel positive energy emanating from this situation?

Due to the health challenges I have faced, there has been a need to continuously address parts of my life that may be draining my energy. Once identified, I am able to immediately resolve them by taking action. If the negative energy comes from a person in my life, I will talk to them about how important it is for me to maintain positive relationships that bring me energy. I cannot hold on to relationships that are draining; I know that I simply don't have any energy reserves to waste.

For a chronically negative relationship, I immediately put change into place. After explaining my needs and why these changes are important to me, along with working with the other person on solutions to create a relationship that is positive for the both of us, I put the situation in their hands. No one is perfect, but if a pattern arises, it needs to be addressed in a loving and compassionate way.

If they do not make necessary changes and are not making an effort to establish a positive, healthy environment, I simply have to release that relationship. Or, at the very least, I will need to drastically limit my exposure to them. When your health is at stake, the relationships in your life need to lift you up—don't ever feel bad about that.

This is also true in regards to your living environment. Make sure to take inventory of both your physical and emotional surroundings, and trim away the excess if necessary!

20) Social Time

The Great Enricher

66*Cheerfulness is the atmosphere in which all things thrive.*99

– Jean Paul Richter

There is an incredible amount of energy to be found in the relationships we develop. Finding people that make you see the world in a new light, who challenge and inspire you, and who cause you to let out your sincerest laugh can lead to the kind of joy that makes you spring from bed in the morning. Just as negative relationships can drain us of energy, positive ones can cause us to grow in ways we never considered possible. So, please feel my excitement as I tell you, get out there and be social! Explore new friendships, try new outlets, and bring people into your life that will help you be the best and happiest version of you.

Isolation can be a slippery slope, and it is easy for the world to seem dangerous when we feel like we are alone. This is why it is so important to make a conscious effort to regularly connect with others.

When loneliness begins to creep in, make it a point to call a friend to join you for lunch, a walk, or even just to enjoy a little tea in the afternoon. Check your calendar often to make sure you are scheduling time for the people in your life.

Make your interactions about kindness and compassion. According to Dr. David Hamilton, these two virtues can physically impact our blood vessels for the better. The positive changes we make to our world translate directly over to our physical health. So, be sure to make them wonderful!

21) You Are the Miracle

The Greatest One of All—You!

66*You already have the precious mixture
that will make you well.*99

– Rumi

I love this quote by Rumi, because it emphasizes a stunning truth - we can search the whole world over for a miracle cure, but it isn't until we look inside that we realize *we are the miracle*. We have more power inside of us than most people will ever realize or come to know within their lifetimes.

Choose from any of the tools and practices listed in this Wave and watch in wonder as the rewards start to flow. Each of them will enrich your life, help you cope with stress, and bring about a greater sense of peace.

What we put into our bodies, the thoughts we allow a place in our minds, how we live each and every day, and the relationships we have all have an enormous effect on our health. The part of self-care that needs to be a part of your daily regime is to always remember to wrap yourself in love. You are a miracle, and by recognizing that, your joy will abound.

Love Changes Everything

During one of my appointments with my holistic practitioner, he mentioned to me that my cells needed to relearn how to be healthy. Looking back, I am astounded and humbled by the amazing changes that love has inspired in my own health and well-being. I know that flooding my system with love and letting my energy levels come alive with the help of positive thoughts, I have been witness to a miraculous transformation in my body.

I am so grateful and honored to share all of these experiences with you! Just as my life was transformed through the power of love, I believe that you have an opportunity to do the same. Fall madly in love with who you are, and your health will respond. Let love in, and then watch as it radiates out and covers your world.

Spreading the Blessings

A Deep and Profound Gratitude

66*What matters most is that we live a life of excellence and be in a position to realize our dreams.*99

– Kathryn Ford

As I write the final pages of this book, let me say that I am so very blessed to be thriving and living a life of excellence. I am deeply grateful that, by practicing the many techniques that focus on health and wellness, the cycle of love in and love out continues.

Let me also say, it has been my honor and privilege to have been able to share a segment of my personal journey with you. It has been a transformational experience for me writing and living it, and I hope it has inspired you with the potential of what your life could be. I want you to not only survive every one of the challenges you may face, but also to thrive through—and because of—those experiences.

At *Excellence Institute*, we coach, mentor, support, and guide our clients towards living a life of excellence and realizing their dreams. We are privileged to support people all over the world, and I would like to invite you to contact me through my website, http://www.kathrynford.com, if you would like my personal support as you walk down your own path to excellence.

On my website, you will find resources in the way of articles I have written, access to my *Be Well! Daily Affirmations*, and other free wellness gifts. My hope is that each one of them will help you on your own journey to making the rest of your life the best of your life. If you have the opportunity to attend one of my speaking engagements, please come up and introduce yourself. I can't wait to meet you!

Here's to your best life!

Surrounding you with love and light – Kathryn

Case Studies

In This Section

* Client Interviews and Feedback

❝Kathryn has taught me how to respond to circumstances, rather than just reacting to them.❞

– Martin Spangler

What My Clients Say...

I have been blessed to have a wide range of clients, who come from a variety of backgrounds, and are facing all kinds of life challenges. I love them dearly, and I hold a special place in my heart for each and every one of them. I am so blessed to have the opportunity to share success stories from four amazing clients. Hopefully this will give you a taste of the experiences they had while working with me and creating a new and better life for themselves. Enjoy!

Client Interview: 1

Sara Sterkel

> **❝***If nothing ever changed, there'd be no butterflies.***❞**
>
> Unknown

Prior to being coached by Kathryn, I had no real sense of myself and lacked a sense of deserving, always seeking approval and validation from others. I did not take care of myself physically or emotionally.

Somehow, I developed the idea that I was not worthy, and my lack of caring for my health and well-being reflected this. I realize now that I was very negative and hopeless, in addition to being extremely dependent upon others. I didn't realize it then, but it was a very self-destructive way of living life; if things were going well, I would actually set myself up for failure, and not success.

The amazing journey with Kathryn was challenging at times, but always insightful, incredibly freeing, and so rewarding as well. She has given me hope and the tools I needed to transform my health and well-being. The number one difference between other therapies I have had in the past, and the coaching, mentoring, and consulting I received from Kathryn, is that she gave me real tools to support me in changing.

Kathryn also provided methods, ideas, and thoughts that helped me move forward to live with a sense of abundance in all areas of my life, such as health, relationships, career and financial freedom, and helped me to move out of living from a sense of lack. Besides all of that, Kathryn was able to shift my focus and thought process on how "thoughts become things," which I found to be very empowering— instead of living from a place of being a victim to circumstances.

Kathryn opened my eyes to a whole new world of vitality and well-being. I am in a much better place, and with so many hopes and dreams now for myself that I didn't have before. I have priceless inner peace and a deep knowing that it's really okay if people don't feel the same way as I do. It's okay, since I am happy with myself as a person.

Kathryn has taught me so much, but practicing the "art of self-care" and shifting my perceptions have been life changing. Regardless of my diagnosis, I now know that I am in control. I now have endless possibilities for living a healthy, happy and fulfilling life!

I love Kathryn's "OCEANS OF WELLNESS'" program, and look forward to continuing to learn and grow, and to move forward in living the life of my dreams! Thank you, Kathryn!

Client Interview: 2

Elissa Simon

66*We delight in the beauty of the butterfly, but rarely admit the changes it has gone through to achieve that beauty.*99

- Maya Angelou

Before I began working with Kathryn, several long-standing issues and unfortunate relationships had been the theme in my life. I had forgotten how to dream. I was just living, not enjoying, or forgiving, or having fun. I felt like I was static or stuck, and not moving forward. I literally felt like I was full of cobwebs, all dusty and dry. I had been in an unproductive place, and was so constricted that my health had fallen apart because of my mind and my toxic thinking patterns.

Then, I began working with Kathryn and things started to move very rapidly. With her support, I began taking back my dreams in order to become the fullest expression of who I really am. My own thinking had become my worst enemy, and I didn't even realize how I was allowing the opinions of others to run my life. Becoming imprisoned in my own mind by other people's opinions of me, along with their rejections of me, criticisms, condemnation, and judgment became the norm. I was ruled by fear.

215

Kathryn took me by the hand, dusted off the cobwebs, and gave me the support I needed to blossom and grow. The work we have done so far together has given me permission to dream again, to grow, and to have the courage to step out and release the patterns and blocks I've had for so many years.

Honestly, I could not have done it without Kathryn. The decision I made to work with her, in order to live a life of excellence, has subsequently changed so many others lives through me, and for the better, too.

I am 65 years old and changing my work in the world, and it was time for me to do something profoundly different. Working with Kathryn has given me the joy back that I had lost along the way. I am heading in a new direction with Kathryn's support, and knowing that she will always be there for me ensures my success. The nurturing of her coaching is so amazing, because she has been through extreme challenges in her own life. I have personally watched her profound transformation and how she has rebounded.

I know she practices the methods, tools, and lifestyle suggestions she teaches, and she is a shining example for all of us! I champion her victory, and it tells me that no one needs to be a victim, no matter what. It showed me we can rise out of the ashes and be glorious. My life has profoundly changed for the better, and I look forward to continuing to work with her, and to taking one quantum leap after another. I love my life and I love you, Kathryn. Thank you!

Client Interview: 3

Martin Spangler

66*Just when the caterpillar thought the world was over, it became a butterfly.*99

– Anonymous

When I first began working with Kathryn, my life was in a downward spiral. I remember one day having the thought that I was emotionally dead. I noticed that and realized it was how I really felt about my life at the time. I felt trapped in a relationship that was dark, and I didn't know how to move through it or get out of it. And then, one year later, I was diagnosed with Stage 4 prostate cancer. It was at that very low point in my life that I knew things needed to change. I needed to shine some light on all of this darkness. It was at that point that I began working with Kathryn.

Kathryn is supportive, compassionate, trustworthy, and an incredible bright light. She taught me how to look beyond my situation and current circumstances, and to focus on what I would love and how I would like my life to be. She taught me how to look for the good feeling thoughts, which brought me to a higher awareness of how much better my life could be.

She also taught me how to respond to circumstances in my life, rather than just react to them. And, she showed me how to connect with the power each of us has within us. Kathryn is a tremendous mentor and consultant, who has been on her own healing journey, and I believe this is one of the reasons she so clearly stands out and above other coaches, mentors, teachers, and consultants.

As a result of adopting Kathryn's practices, principles, methods, and tools, my life has now completely transformed. Negative emotions rarely visit me. I was able to successfully overcome an emotionally abusive marriage of 30 years and be cured of Stage 4 prostate cancer—achieving the best possible outcome with both situations. Today, my life is incredibly rich in every way. I now am truly experiencing a life I love living, and have the necessary tools to continue to create the life of my dreams for the rest of my life!

Client Interview: 4

Christy Hodson

> ❝*How does one become a butterfly? she asked*
> *You must want to fly so much that you are willing*
> *to give up being a caterpillar.*❞
>
> – Trina Paulus

When I found Kathryn, I was experiencing a huge amount of anxiety. Knowing I was to be involuntarily transitioned out of my job was a scary thing for me. In addition to experiencing job loss, I also found myself in the midst of the ending of a six-year relationship, and at the same time becoming one of my mother's primary caregivers. I knew I needed someone to help me to get to the other side. I knew if I had the right tools, I could cross over the bridge and create a more expansive life.

I didn't know how to do this, but I knew I needed a coach to support me and show me how to transform my life. From the beginning, I was open, yet I still had a lot of baggage and emotional discord, including fear of the unknown, which I sorely needed to address. Kathryn's enthusiasm was infectious and I found her to be not only extremely trustworthy, but also sincere, genuine, intelligent, and articulate. From the beginning, she listened to me really well and intently, and I found her to be sincere in relating to me, including the first time we met at a social event where there were a lot of people around us.

At that time, I was in a place of scary transition in regards to my career, healing from a long-term relationship, and dealing with my mom's health. Again, I knew I needed someone to help me get through this, so I asked the Universe to guide and help me. I felt a coach would be the best way, even though I had never been coached before. I don't believe things happen by accident, and I know my meeting Kathryn was, in fact, no accident.

From the start, Kathryn made me feel so good, even though I wasn't sure that I could do it or afford it since I was getting ready to lose my job. I felt a tremendous amount of anxiety due to my job situation, and having to deal with my relationship all in the same time period. But, I was very disciplined in listening to her teachings and doing the corresponding life work. And, I found myself being so excited to have tools!

I now know that the energy I put out, I am going to get back. I also know that I don't have to go through all of this struggle, constant analysis, and come to all these decisions based on my own findings. I've learned through coaching with Kathryn that it can be easy, if I allow it to be. Her coaching has been a transformative process for me, and I know I am a better listener, friend, sister, and daughter as a result.

I am becoming the person I want to attract, and becoming my own best friend, simply by letting go and saying thank you for the lessons. The key for me was when I began being grateful in the moment, and even when I was experiencing a challenge. Kathryn's coaching took my life to a whole new level. And, I feel like I am getting better and better every day.

I respond to circumstances and situations in my life, rather than just reacting. How I respond is especially important as a person and a business woman. I have finally found, and I am now using, my voice. It is okay for me to ask for what I truly desire. It feels so good after a lifetime of being a "people pleaser."

I want to express my truly, truly sincere gratitude to Kathryn, as this is supporting me on a deep level. Internally, I have traveled to multiple continents through this coaching. The richness, depth, adventure, incredible terrain, and open mindedness that we must have as travelers in this work—and by what we see and experience—is all a part of this.

Thank you Kathryn, for inviting me to be a part of this transformative experience. Now I have these tools I can use for the rest of my life. This is something that will live within me forever!

A Personal Invitation for You

Without further ado, it is again my extreme pleasure to invite you to personally come along with me on this fabulous journey of living a life of excellence. I have made the choice to love and live my very best life! You can too. It is a choice, and the most important decision you will ever make.

When I first decided to create my program, *OCEANS OF WELL-NESS* - *A Fountain of Youth*, I was filled with excitement! Not only did it provide me an outlet to help others on a road that I had traveled, but it also allowed me to spread the truth about what we all need in order to live our best life! I invite you to visit my website at http://kathrynford.com to make your personal transformation everything you ever dreamed.

Like I have often heard, "When the student is ready, the teacher will appear." I know that these messages will arrive in your life when you need them most. We are all in this journey together, and I am profoundly honored to share it with you. Thank you for walking hand in hand with me while we absorb all the amazing opportunities and goodness that life has to offer.

About The Author

Kathryn Ford is the Founder and President of *Excellence Institute*, the premier training center for living a life of excellence. She is an award-winning master life coach, consultant, international speaker, and author, specializing in living a life of full-spectrum wealth— wealth that encompasses the three key areas of a life of excellence: health and well-being, which includes your ability to maintain youth-fulness; having an abundance of rich relationships; and freedom of time and money. She is also a "2016 Woman of the Year" nominee for the Los Angeles Business Journal.

Having personally faced 27 years of a chronic medical condition, NMO, Kathryn has successfully navigated the challenges along the way to affect necessary change in her life; this has allowed her to take hold of a life she truly loves. Kathryn lives by the principles she teaches on a daily basis, and is a great example and role model for her clients. These first-hand experiences have allowed her to develop a 7-step system, *OCEANS OF WELLNESS* – *A Fountain of Youth*, for living a life of excellence, no matter what! Her programs have proven to be life-changing.

In 2015, Kathryn was also a featured monthly writer in the inter-national magazine, *Sybil Magazine*. In addition, Kathryn's book, *Be Well! A 7-Step System For Radical Healing*, a #1 Amazon Best Seller was released in September 2016, with the foreword written by Dr. Bernie Siegel. It has been endorsed by some of the world's most influ-ential authorities for personal development and transformation.

Kathryn has an extensive background in coaching and has re-ceived her continuing education from the *Coaching in Leadership and Healthcare* conference, sponsored by Harvard Medical School.

She is also a member of their *Institute of Coaching Professional Association.* Through her coaching programs, Kathryn teaches essential tools and practices for allowing people to live the life of their dreams.

For more information on Kathryn's work, and to enjoy a free gift, go to http://freewellnessgift.com.

50918227R00131

Made in the USA
San Bernardino, CA
07 July 2017